MORE THAN A SEASON

BUILDING A
CHAMPIONSHIP CULTURE

DAYTON MOORE

WITH

MATT FULKS

TRIUMPH
B O O K S

TRIUMPHBOOKS.COM

This book is available in quantity at special discounts for your group or organization. For further information, contact:

Triumph Books LLC
814 North Franklin Street
Chicago, Illinois 60610
(312) 337-0747
www.triumphbooks.com

Printed in U.S.A.
ISBN: 978-1-62937-155-9
Editorial production by Alex Lubertozzi
Photos courtesy of Kansas City Royals unless otherwise noted

To Marianne, who's a source of constant love, support, encouragement, and wise counsel. You have helped mold me into who I am today. To our three children, Ashley, Avery, and Robert, who make me proud every day to be your father. One of my core beliefs is that my team is at home— I couldn't imagine this journey without the four of you. To my in-laws, James and Christine Bixler, who are great sources of faith, confidence, and strength. To my brother and sister, Duke and Danielle, who are great fans of the Royals and make me proud to be your brother. To my grandmother, Wynona (Riner) Marley, who helped foster my love of the Royals at an early age. To my grandfather, Cecil Marley, who became a huge Royals fan after I became general manager, and passed away at the age of 98 before Game 3 of the 2014 World Series. To my father and mother, Robert and Penne, who supported and encouraged me to pursue this great game of baseball.

CONTENTS

Acknowledgments   vii
Foreword by *Alex Gordon*   xi
Introduction by *William F. High*   xvii

1 90 FEET AWAY   1
2 A MIDWESTERN KID REALIZES HIS DREAM   9
3 A BRAVE NEW WORLD   32
4 "YOU CAN'T WIN IN KANSAS CITY"   50
5 CHANGING THE CULTURE   66
6 ORGANIZATIONAL HARMONY   98
7 THE PROCESS   109
8 THE PRODIGAL SON RETURNS   131
9 OPERATION: FLIP THE SWITCH   148
10 THE PROCESS COMES TO FRUITION   170

Appendices:
    C You in the Major Leagues   197
    "Dear Dayton . . ."   199

ACKNOWLEDGMENTS

AS ALWAYS, IT SEEMS like there are too many people to thank, because there's no way a book can be completed without a great amount of support and assistance. That said, we apologize now if we forget to mention you by name. The following people were incredibly instrumental in the authors' being able to write this book:

To the team at Triumph Books, who believed in this project, were willing to squeeze it onto their roster, and then showed the patience of Job as this book became a reality: Noah Amstadter, Jeff Fedotin, Alex Lubertozzi, and Mitch Rogatz.

To Bill High of the National Christian Foundation Heartland, who convinced Dayton that this would be a worthwhile project, and then wrote the book's introduction.

To Alex Gordon for agreeing to write the foreword. You can read more about Alex later in the book, but besides being a terrific baseball player, Alex is a great person.

To each person who agreed to be interviewed for the book: George Brett, Jeff Davenport, Bill Fischer, David Glass, Rusty Kuntz, Nick Leto, John Schuerholz, Paul Snyder, Art Stewart, Gene Watson, and Donnie Williams. Thank you for your time and willingness to share your thoughts. There are many others who could've shared stories about Dayton and his time with both the Braves and the Royals, but the ones we talked with offer a solid backdrop of Dayton's time in Atlanta and Kansas City.

To Colby Curry and Mike Swanson in the Royals media relations department, for your support and assistance with photos and information. Along those lines, to photographers Don Schmidt and Chris Vleisides. To Brad Hainje with the Braves and Greg Piduch with George Mason University, for helping secure photos.

To Emily Penning, Dayton's assistant, whose contributions to this project are immeasurable, from setting up interviews, to helping with contacts, to offering suggestions, to making a mean turkey sandwich. As Dayton says, Emily has a tireless work ethic with an above-and-beyond attitude.

To Dave and Kathy Minich for giving Matt a hideaway in the middle of Missouri so he could work on this project.

Dayton would like to add a personal thanks:

To my college coaches, Joe Slobko and Billy Brown, who gave me an opportunity to continue playing and then fostered my desire to get into coaching.

To my mentors and encouragers in this business: Paul Snyder, Roy Clark, John Schuerholz, Donnie Williams, Bill Fischer, Jose Martinez, Jim Beauchamp, Chino Cadahia, and Art Stewart. As we write later in the book, it's important to have "gray-haired" influences, and these men certainly embody that for me.

To each player with whom I've shared this incredible baseball journey. It takes a lot of dedication to play this game, and I've been blessed to be around passionate baseball men who love to compete. Every player's story begins with a scout. So, I thank the scouts, who are the lifeblood of the game, as well as each manager, coach, and instructor who supports, encourages, and prepares our players to be their very best.

To Dr. Vincent Key and the entire medical team at KU Medical Center, our head athletic trainer Nick Kenney, assistant trainer Kyle Turner, strength and conditioning coach Ryan Stoneberg, and physical therapist Jeff Blum, all of whom keep our players in the best possible shape and health to perform their best.

To the leaders throughout our baseball operations department whose hard work, dedication to the Royals, wise counsel, and passion to see players reach their ceilings is something on which I've depended, in particular: Dean Taylor, J.J. Picollo, Rene Francisco, Jin Wong, Lonnie Goldberg, Scott Sharp, Gene Watson, Mike Groopman, Mike Arbuckle, Linda Smith, George Brett, and Jason Kendall. Along those lines, thank you to the spouses and families of the people in our baseball operations department.

To the Glass family, particularly David and Dan, who entrusted me with this job of general manager and then showed patience to allow us to see the plan through.

To Tim Cash and Pastor Christian Newsome, who are spiritual mentors and friends. You are wonderful examples of Christ to me and so many others.

To Marianne and our three children, Ashley, Avery, and Robert, who are never-ending sources of joy and encouragement. Your support is appreciated more than you'll ever know.

Finally, from Matt:

Thanks to Dayton for thinking I could pull off this project. The call I received the week of Thanksgiving and the two-plus months that followed will always be one of the highlights of my career. We shared a lot of laughs, a lot of discussions, and a lot of coffee, but I'm a better writer and a better person because of our time together.

To Marianne, thank you for your hospitality, willingness to offer editorial suggestions, and encouragement during this project.

To Jim Wissel, Chris Browne, Tom Lawrence, and Tim and Amy Brown, who, as always, served as core support and guidance. Your support is greatly appreciated!

As with past book projects, based on the amount of praying I did during the writing of this, especially during the last two weeks, without Christ this isn't possible.

A final special thanks to my favorite in-laws, Todd and Pat Burwell, and my parents, Fred and Sharon. To Helen, Charlie, and Aaron, who make me thankful each day; and, to my best friend, Libby, who loves me in spite of my quirkiness and shows me that it takes a special person to live with an author on deadline.

Thank you, all.

FOREWORD

WHAT A DIFFERENCE a couple of seasons can make. Two years after losing 90 games in 2012, we were American League champions for only the third time in Royals history and 90 feet away from tying Game 7 of the World Series in the bottom of the ninth inning. It's been an incredible roller coaster.

There were a lot of ups and downs in those three seasons alone, not to mention the years before that. We lost 91 games in 2011. So, after back-to-back 90-loss seasons, we were in range of a playoff berth in 2013 until the last few days of the season. Our record of 86–76 in 2013 was the first winning season for the Royals in a decade, and the most wins in a season for the club since 1989.

The architect behind this turnaround is general manager Dayton Moore, who's been my boss since he started with the Royals in June 2006.

At that time I was at Double A Wichita, in my first full season playing for the organization. I'll never forget the buzz around the clubhouse when he came down to see us for the first time. We drew only about two hundred people a game in Wichita, so any type of excitement around the stadium was great. Hearing that Dayton Moore was coming to see us really fired a lot of guys up.

There wasn't really a lot of nervousness knowing that we'd be meeting him for the first time and that he'd be watching us play. Initially, that's probably because we were a bunch of 20- to 24-year-old kids who didn't know any better. We were just out there having fun playing baseball. Once you meet Dayton, though, you realize there's no reason to be nervous around him — he puts people at ease quickly.

When you're around Dayton you learn pretty fast what's important to him. Sure, he's highly competitive, so winning is near the top of his list. Higher on the list, though, are his faith and people, specifically his family. Dayton is an amazing family man to his wife, Marianne, and their three kids, Ashley, Avery, and Robert.

That feeling of family extends to us as players and the people throughout baseball operations for the Royals. He is a father figure who knows how to get the most out of the people around him, and he always says the right thing at the perfect time. One example of that for me was in 2010 when I was being sent down to Triple A Omaha after being in the majors for three years. Not only were they sending me to Omaha, they wanted to convert me to an outfielder.

That was a challenging time in my life. I came up in 2007 as a third baseman but fought a couple of injuries and ended up having hip surgery in 2009. I struggled after coming back from that, and I wasn't playing nearly as well as I felt I should've been. In the minors, Mike Moustakas was tearing things up and looked like the club's future third baseman. On May 2 in Tampa Bay, Dayton and then-manager Trey Hillman talked to me about going to Omaha. During that conversation, Dayton told me that I was still part of this organization's future and turning things around. It was obvious that it wasn't just GM talk to make me feel better. It was reassuring to hear that from him.

From what I understand, the club discussed moving me to outfield early in my career when Mark Teahen was at third and I was at Wichita. For whatever reason, they left me at third and moved Mark to the outfield. Looking back now, if they had moved me then, I'm not sure I would've become a Gold Glove outfielder. The position change was something I needed because it gave me a new obstacle to focus on. It was fun and exciting. Frankly, I'm glad Dayton decided to do it. It's definitely true that everything happens for a reason.

That moment is why I can say without hesitation that Dayton genuinely cares for each player on and off the field. He wants us to make good decisions and not embarrass the organization, but it's also about our lives as individuals. Because of the interest he shows in us, he is highly respected in our clubhouse. Everyone looks up to him.

Dayton is a strong leader who's always positive. That's a good quality to have when you're trying to lead 25 guys in the clubhouse of a sport where you're going to fail more often than succeed. Organizations—even corporations—tend to take the shape and attitude of their leader. When the leader has Dayton's positive outlook, it filters down to everyone else in an encouraging way.

But it's not only his attitude. Dayton is extremely focused. Look at the eight years it took to build our club into a World Series team. When he took the job, the team was losing 100 games a year. That's a tough situation to come into and be expected to win quickly. Dayton came in with a mindset of how he was going to do it and then stuck with the plan, even through all the naysayers. Plenty of people were saying that he was doing it the wrong way or that he was failing, but he remained focused on the process. That term—*process*—was mocked, but that's how he built the team: drafting talented players, bringing them through the system, signing or trading for major league guys, and then seeing more young players come from the minors. Even though people didn't think it was working, as players we could see it coming together.

As a player you know when you see talented players and great athletes. So we understood what he was doing when he made great trades that people didn't agree with, especially the one with Milwaukee that brought Lorenzo Cain and Alcides Escobar for Zack Greinke, and the one with Tampa Bay that brought James Shields and Wade Davis in exchange for several players, including Wil Myers. Dayton brought the right pieces in, and we all jelled. We also saw behind the scenes what was going on in the minor leagues. Everyone can now see the fruits of Dayton's hard work.

From our minor league system, Billy Butler and I were here already, and then Eric Hosmer, Mike Moustakas, Salvador Perez, and others were in that second wave. When I was sent down to Omaha in 2010, I saw the talent firsthand in the minor leagues, which motivated me to work a little harder to get back up with these guys. Now another group of players is getting major league ready in the minors.

Don't get me wrong, it's been a long process. There have been a lot of downs that Dayton and I, along with the organization, had to go through to get to the point where we are now. I had success everywhere I played growing up, through my time at the University of Nebraska, but I struggled when I got called up to Kansas City and didn't know how to deal with it. Dayton was one of the people who helped me get through it. To get to where we were in 2014, all of the struggles and negative talk about Dayton and the club seem worth it. It was an indescribable feeling to share the experience with Dayton along with guys like Billy Butler and Luke Hochevar, who were with the organization since the transformation began.

More Than a Season is the perfect title for this book because, for Dayton Moore, life is about more than what happens during the course of a season. Obviously, it would've been incredible to win the 2014 World Series, but whether we won or lost, Dayton was going to be the same person. He is a great, humble man with outstanding character.

Not everyone is lucky enough to have a boss who is both a genuinely good person and an outstanding leader. The following pages will give you a better understanding of where he came from and how he built the Royals from a 100-loss team to American League champions.

Regardless of what happens throughout the rest of my career and after, it'll always be an honor to say that I played for Kansas City and Dayton Moore.

— Alex Gordon

INTRODUCTION

"WHY DO YOU STILL ENJOY doing this work after all these years?" Her question was honest and simple, yet valid. She was interviewing for a job but wanted to know why I'm still doing the same thing after nearly 15 years.

The answer was equally simple: "*It's the stories. I love to hear the stories of people, their pain, their joy, and how those stories connect with one another and ultimately the Divine Story.*"

Dayton Moore's story is one of those. His story is one of a simple, straightforward, Midwestern guy with a love and passion for the game of baseball. But it's more than baseball—a lot more.

Even though he's reached one of the highest levels in sports, been to the World Series, and he gets to hang out with world-class athletes in a multibillion-dollar sport, none of that seems to faze Dayton.

One of the best stories that illustrates what I mean didn't come from Dayton. I was having coffee with Kevin Seitzer, the former Royals hitting coach who's now the Atlanta Braves hitting coach. Kevin relayed how it was one of those picture-perfect days with blue sky and fresh spring breeze. Twelve-year-olds patrolled the outfield while Dayton hit lazy fly balls to an eager group. In the afternoon sun, Dayton paused, leaned in on the bat, and wistfully remarked, "It doesn't get any better than this."

That's Dayton Moore—a man with a love for a game. He loves baseball but he also loves to coach, to teach, to inspire a dream—whether it's a 12-year-old kid on a diamond or a 22-year-old in a classroom.

So when I first met Dayton, it's no surprise that our conversation didn't focus on him or his experiences in baseball. We probably discussed 45 things in 30 minutes, touching on family, baseball, ministry, leadership, and the community. It was a fun, fast-paced conversation.

Most of all Dayton wanted to talk about helping people—those in need, those who needed to be inspired and to live beyond what they thought possible. He talked about his goal to establish a foundation called "C You in the Major Leagues." The foundation would help kids who wouldn't have a chance to play competitive baseball without its support. The foundation wouldn't just stop there, however. It was about creating opportunities for students and others in need.

So that's what we did. We formally established the C You in the Major Leagues Foundation through the National Christian Foundation Heartland. It was an extension of what Dayton had already been doing informally, but this provided structure. In keeping with Dayton's personality, many of the gifts from the foundation have been anonymous. In his first public launch of the foundation, more than 150 people came out to hear the dream of the foundation.

There's more to come. Dayton thinks big. He's been involved in the community—helping the homeless, speaking to business owners, leading camps, and encouraging pastoral leaders. He wants to make the community better. He wants to help people.

So it shouldn't come as a surprise that when a few people, including me, mentioned to Dayton that he should write a book, he was reluctant. For him it's about focusing on the team and on others, not on himself. When he realized he could write a book that shares his journey and the lessons he's learned along the way, he was on board. Notably, none of his proceeds from this book go to Dayton. All the profits from the book go to his foundation, so that more good can be accomplished.

In the coming pages of *More Than a Season*, you'll read and hear of the journey of a man, and the lessons he's learned along the way in building a championship culture. You don't have to like baseball, either, to enjoy this book. Instead, you'll capture the idea that life is built so much on the ideas of persistence, character, and faith. As we all grab those ideas, then, well, in Dayton's words, "It doesn't get any better than this."

—William F. High
CEO/President
National Christian Foundation Heartland

CHAPTER 1
90 FEET AWAY

BASEBALL IS A GAME OF INCHES. It's a tough game. It's a game of failure. But it is also very rewarding.

The 2014 Kansas City Royals experienced all of these things during a 29-day postseason stretch, culminating with Game 7 of the World Series. It all started with the wild-card game against Oakland (see chapter 10 for more on that). Inches separated us from the end of the season and a trip to Anaheim on Salvador Perez's game-winning bouncer down the left-field line. There we were, though, a month later, playing in Game 7 of the World Series.

Going into the seventh game against the San Francisco Giants, I felt confident that we would win it, especially coming off a 10–0 win in Game 6 the night before. After what we'd seen during the entire postseason run, as Game 7 went on, even with the way Giants pitcher Madison Bumgarner was throwing in late-inning relief, I thought that, if we could get a runner, we could get him across the plate. Why wouldn't any of us think that way? If we learned nothing else during the postseason, it was that this was a resilient bunch of Royals that had learned how to overcome deficits late in games. The common theme of that whole group was that they absolutely loved to play baseball, which made them tough and resilient.

Salvador Perez, a good bad-ball hitter, pulls a low and outside pitch from Oakland's Jason Hammel past the third baseman in the 12th inning of the wild-card game that sent us into an incredible October 2014.

There was a sense early in Game 7 that the magic might continue. After the Giants scored first with two runs in the top of the second off starter Jeremy Guthrie, we came right back with two runs in the bottom of the inning. That was it for the Royals. The Giants took the lead for good with a run in the fourth. San Francisco manager Bruce Bochy turned to his ace, Bumgarner, in the fifth. But just when it looked like the Royals were finished with two outs in the bottom of the ninth, Alex Gordon drove a ball to left-center. Gregor Blanco, whom I've known since he was 16, misplayed the ball, and it rolled to the wall. Juan Perez then bobbled the ball as he tried to pick it up. At that moment, a part of me thought Gordo had a chance to make it all the way home. However, from where I was sitting, I had a direct line of the relay. Third-base coach Mike Jirschele stopped Gordo at third as shortstop Brandon Crawford was about to get the relay throw in shallow left-center from Perez. Crawford was the key person on the play for two reasons. One, he has one of the best arms for a shortstop in major league baseball. Two, because of how deep he went to retrieve the relay, it's a much tougher decision for the third-base coach.

As fun as it would've been to see Alex try to score there, if I'm Jirsch, I'm making the same call of stopping Alex, mainly because of Crawford's arm. I thought Salvador Perez, who was on deck, would get a hit just like he did against Oakland about a month earlier. Salvy, who was going to be aggressive, is a good bad-ball hitter, and Bumgarner's pitches were in and out of the zone. If Salvy gets a hit, Gordo ties it, we pinch-run for Salvy, and then who knows what happens with Mike Moustakas coming up. Unfortunately, it didn't happen. We were 90 feet away.

After the season, I was privileged, along with Alex, to be part of turning on the Christmas lights at Kansas City's famous Country Club Plaza. One of the local media personalities saw us backstage and razzed Gordo a little about not trying to score.

"Do you know our third-base coach's name?" I asked the TV personality.

"No, I don't."

"Well, if Alex had kept running and gotten thrown out at the plate, you and everyone else in the country would've known it for the wrong reason. Mike Jirschele, who's an excellent third-base coach, would've gone down in World Series history for making that mistake."

The other big discussion right after the series, and rightly so, was Bumgarner. He turned in one of the most impressive performances in World Series history in 2014 by winning two games, saving one, and seeing his World Series ERA drop to 0.25. Because of all of that he was selected as the World Series MVP. Bumgarner is a true "giant" with a great ability to pitch and a great heart to compete. When your best players are your team's best competitors, you always have a chance to win. That's what Madison Bumgarner brought to that San Francisco team during the World Series.

After the game, I went down to our clubhouse, which was quiet except for reporters interviewing players, and I walked around to the players and coaches and thanked each one for their hard work and dedication to the Royals. I told them how proud of them we were as an organization and as a city.

That group of men helped reignite a baseball passion in Kansas City. Frankly, one of the things I enjoyed most with that postseason run was the joy that winning brought to our city and the way it united people. We lost more than a generation of fans because we weren't winning. Kids and grandkids were becoming Red Sox and Braves and Yankees fans because those teams were winning. As a parent of baseball fans, you want your kids to experience the great things — the winning, the civic pride, the fun games — that you experienced. To see that come around and then to receive letters or hear comments from someone as I stand in line at a coffee shop, or to read of people drawing encouragement from our club as they battled cancer and other potentially deadly diseases, is incredibly uplifting.

I tried to be positive around everyone, including the players, coaches, and manager Ned Yost in the clubhouse, but it was tough to feel anything but completely dejected. My emotions did get the better of me later that night.

As I was driving home, Gene Watson, our director of professional scouting, whom I've known since our Atlanta days, called me.

"Well, it was a great season," he said.

"Great, Gene? What's so great about it? I understand what you're saying, but what's so great about it? We had an opportunity to win the World Series and we didn't."

I continued to vent. I knew it wasn't the right thing to do, but that's part of the emotions you go through after losing the World Series. For that moment, maybe I wore my emotions a little louder because of how we lost and knowing how close we were at the end. Don't get me wrong: I was grateful and appreciative toward the players and the leaders throughout our organization who helped us reach that point, but I was wrapped up in the moment. Everyone manages failure differently. As you'll read several times throughout this book, the key to baseball is who manages failure the best. You will fail in baseball. Period. But the people and teams that manage it the best are able to reach their ceilings.

I didn't handle it the way I would've liked after Game 7. There was a lot of frustration and hurt that we didn't win. And, perhaps, selfishness and pride on my part—wanting to be the general manager of a World Series championship team—made me react the way I did to Gene. It was competitiveness in me, but it was a human flaw to react that harshly to our director of professional scouting. Taking it a step further, Gene was a big reason we made a particular move that helped us get to the World Series. As you'll read more in-depth later, he was the one who orchestrated the James Shields and Wade Davis trade and then kept me motivated to make the move. We didn't want to trade Wil Myers, but based on our plan and how we needed to get there, we needed to trade Wil and others for Shields and Davis. That turned out to be a blessing for our franchise, and it's a huge credit to Gene.

Later, I called Gene and apologized for the way I spoke to him. We all need people in our lives who can be sounding boards for our true feelings and emotions, in good times and in bad. For me, Gene Watson is one of those people.

o o o

Losing a World Series, whether you're expected to be there or not, hurts. After Game 7, it felt as if Yordano Ventura or Kelvin Herrera hit me in the gut with a fastball. Working for the Atlanta Braves taught me how hard it is to get to the World Series, let alone win it. And we were doing it there with three Hall of Fame pitchers in Greg Maddux, Tom Glavine, and John Smoltz, future Hall of Fame player Chipper Jones, and Hall of Fame manager Bobby Cox. So I understood this was a special opportunity. I wanted to try to enjoy every moment, but as a competitor and a general manager, I couldn't help but gravitate toward the thoughts, *How are we going to do this again? What do we have to do next year?*

Regardless of your field, those questions apply to all of us, especially when you've been 90 feet away from your

It was a long process from June 2006 until that word "Postseason" was on the wall behind me in our dugout in 2014, but I'm so happy for our players, our organization, and all of our fans.

goal. How are we going to do this again? And what do we have to do to get better next year?

There have been many times in my life when I've been only 90 feet away. Other times I've crossed home plate. The following pages are about those times for me and how we brought this once proud Kansas City Royals club from a 100-loss franchise to within 90 feet of tying Game 7 in the bottom of the ninth inning of the 2014 World Series.

o o o

As I pulled into the driveway after talking with Gene Watson a few hours after Perez ended Game 7 by popping out to third baseman Pablo Sandoval, I was reminded of the most vivid images from the 2014 postseason run: *my* home team—my family. Our first three or four years in Kansas City were difficult on our entire family. It was a challenge for us as a family to weather the criticism that was directed toward the Royals and, ultimately, me as the general manager. There were many times I wanted to fight back with and through the media, but I wisely shut my mouth and stayed focused on our long-term plan. There's no way I could have gotten through that time without a strong faith system and my wife, Marianne, who's always been a great encourager to me. To see her and our three kids—Ashley, Avery, and Robert—enjoy the 2014 post-season run after what they endured in previous years is rewarding and special.

That's where it begins and ends with me: family. As much as I love the Kansas City Royals and our people within the organization, my favorite team is at home. I've always strived to make them a priority, second only to my relationship with Christ. That love and commitment and importance of family was shown to me throughout my entire life.

CHAPTER 2
A MIDWESTERN KID REALIZES HIS DREAM

EVER SINCE I PICKED UP a baseball, or at least since being introduced to the sport, there hasn't been a day when I didn't think about baseball. I've been in love with the game for as long as I can remember.

Growing up in the 1970s, many of us could imagine ourselves reaching baseball's biggest stage, the World Series, and getting the game-winning hit in Game 7. We all created those situations as kids. For me it was a passion as much as it was a dream. As kids in western New York, we'd play Wiffle ball, tennis ball, or one on-one as we pitched to the strike zone painted on the side of our elementary school. We'd go through the Royals lineup as they faced the Dodgers or whichever team seemed to be a good opponent. Except the Yankees. It was never the Yankees. We read the box scores every day so we could recite the lineups better than we could Bible verses. We shared a lot of dreams about playing in the big leagues. The only way to get there, we thought then, was to win the day. Be the best you can be each day. As with life, we'd start with a fresh slate each day.

And, yes, you read that previous paragraph correctly. It was almost always the Kansas City Royals against someone else. The Royals were my team, thanks to my parents' roots and, especially, my grandmother's love of the team.

o o o

My mother, Penne, grew up in Coldwater, Kansas, which is a wheat farming community about two hours west of Wichita, Kansas. In the mid-1960s, she was attending a small business school in Wichita when some mutual friends introduced her to Robert Moore, who had served on the USS *Yorktown* during Vietnam but was working at Beechcraft, an airline manufacturing company based in Wichita. There must've been an instant attraction between Robert and Penne because they dated about three months before getting married. My brother, sister, and I were all born in Wichita a few years later. I was the oldest, followed by Duke about three years later, and then Danielle about three years after him. Shortly after Danielle was born when I was in kindergarten, we moved to Lakewood, New York, when Dad took a job with Chautauqua Airlines.

Every August we'd spend two to three weeks with my grandparents in Coldwater. That's where I developed a love for the Royals because my grandmother, Wynona, was a huge fan. With our mutual love of baseball and my love for my grandmother, baseball and the Royals became easy topics of conversation for us. If we weren't listening to Buddy Blattner, Denny Matthews, and Fred White on the radio, we were staying up late to see the score on the news. The next morning, we'd grab the newspaper and head directly for the previous night's box score. The Royals were an easy team for me to like because they were winning and made it to the playoffs seemingly every year.

One of those playoff moments remains burned on my mind. In 1976, the Royals' first time going to the postseason, they were tied with the Yankees, two games to two, in a best-of-five series. We were watching in the bottom of the ninth, with the game tied at 6–6, when Chris Chambliss hit a walk-off home run over the right-field wall at Yankee Stadium. I started bawling. And bawling. Unfortunately, that's one of my earliest Royals memories.

Another Royals memory that is extremely vivid for a much better reason was nine years later. I was a freshman at Garden City Community College and I had spent fall break with Dave Larson, a teammate of mine, in Illinois. Our drive back to Garden City, Kansas, happened to be on the same day as Game 7 of the 1985 World Series. Being somewhat naïve college freshmen, we thought we could stop at then–Royals Stadium and buy tickets for the game against the St. Louis Cardinals. Of course the game was sold out—and we couldn't afford the tickets anyway—but we noticed there were a lot of people parked on Interstate 70, watching the game from a grassy area between the stadium and the interstate. So we decided to join them. From that spot we could see everything except Lonnie Smith in left field. It was an absolute blast! One of the people had a portable television, so we could tell exactly what was going on. To this day, thinking about the crowd's electricity that we could feel near I-70 still gives me chills.

o o o

While I was attending Lakewood Elementary School, I continued to play baseball in the spring and summer, but the sport that wrested some of my attention away from baseball was hockey. I was on a traveling team that played in tournaments throughout New York and even in Canada. Of course, excitement surrounding the sport grew during that time with the 1980 U.S. Olympic men's hockey team's "Miracle on Ice" about seven hours up the road in Lake Placid. I didn't have the same love for hockey as I did baseball, but it's a fascinating sport to most people. The hand-eye coordination needed in hockey rivals that of hitting a baseball. Royals Hall of Fame broadcaster Denny Matthews, who's a hockey connoisseur, summed up hockey perfectly: "Hockey is a fast, instinctive game. There's also no foul territory, so once you're on the rink, you can't run out of bounds to avoid a hit…. The most intriguing part of it is playing on a foreign surface."

Any thoughts I might've had of becoming the next Bobby Hull or Guy Lafleur were dashed after the eighth grade when Dad took a job with Mississippi Valley Airlines and we moved to Moline, Illinois, where the closest hockey league was more than an hour away in Peoria.

Each new job my father took meant a move to another city and the instability that might bring to a family. But he was doing it to improve our family's situation. The move to Illinois certainly did that. Before going to Moline, my mother worked outside the home to help make ends meet, even though it was unusual at that time for women to work. We weren't poor, but there were mornings we'd wake up without milk in the house. Neither of my parents had a college degree, and we were what one might consider a blue-collar family.

From the examples set by my parents, though, I learned so many incredible life lessons that molded who I am today. Although we moved a lot, my father worked extremely hard, from morning until night. He would recite a rhyme to us kids that still rings in my head today: "Do a job, big or small, do it right or not at all." When I first got into coaching, he would say, "You need to work every job like it's the last one you'll ever have." He treated people with kindness. He was both respectful and respected, and showed what it meant to be transparent. Then there was my mother who was a very tough Midwestern woman who was never afraid to speak her mind. And she was a tough, unbelievable competitor. At her funeral, one woman said, "Penne Moore was the toughest woman I've ever met in my life." That was true. She'd drop the gloves in a heartbeat. Dad was the spiritual leader of the family. He made sure we were in church as much as possible as a family, which was an important component that he was trying to instill in the family.

Dad also helped coach my teams in New York, but sports weren't a huge part of my parents' childhoods because both worked on their family's farms growing up. Besides the overall passion I had for hockey and baseball, with all of the moving we did as a family, the best way for me to make new friends was through sports. As kids we get a lot of our identity and self-esteem from sports. After my sophomore year of high school, that identity came mainly from baseball. Academics weren't high on my list, and I dropped all other sports because my passion to learn the game of baseball was so intense. When I was 15, I started charting *Monday Night Baseball* games. And then, each October I would tape playoff games on our VCR and watch them all winter.

Our teams were passionate about winning. Before my senior year of high school, our American Legion team was the first team from Moline to reach the Great Lakes Regional tournament, which was played that year in

Rapid City, South Dakota. My coach told me after one of our games that a Royals scout wanted to meet me. I was stunned. In those days we didn't see a lot of scouts, but a scout for the Royals—*my* team—wanted to meet me? That was a dream come true.

That scout's name was Art Stewart. The way he made me feel was something I'll never forget. He made a great impression on me. I always think back to that, anytime I meet a young player. He asked questions about my interests and about my family. He praised me for the way I played the game, hustled, and the intensity I showed on the field. I'm not sure if he remembers the conversation, but I certainly do. From meeting him that day as a 17-year-old and then crossing paths during the years I was with the Braves, working with Art was one of the things I looked forward to the most when I took the job with the Royals more than 20 years later.

> I definitely remember it. Dayton was a fiery shortstop; a pepper pot. Boy, he was an impressive shortstop. He played extremely well in that tournament. After the game I stopped him and said, "Young man, you got a minute?" I told him who I was and said, "I have an information card here. Would you mind filling it out?" Needless to say, he was elated to do it.
>
> —Art Stewart

My baseball focus has changed since those days of dreaming of a major league playing career, but there remains something magical about a bat and a ball. I was blessed to play on good teams, which added to my obsession with winning. It's been channeled as I've matured to a passion for team excellence, doing things the right way, bringing honor to the organization and people who have believed in me, and bringing honor to God.

But my journey in the game was far from being over.

"THAT RUN'S ON YOU, MOORE!"

During my senior year of high school, with my sights set on continuing my baseball career at the University of Missouri, I went to a Cincinnati Reds tryout camp. Larry Smith, a Reds scout, came up to me and asked where I was going to school.

"I'm thinking about going to the University of Missouri," I said with a tone that told him my options were still open, especially if I had a chance to sign a professional contract.

"You won't play if you go there because Dave Silvestri will be the starting shortstop there this year," he said. "There's a junior college in Kansas I'd like you to think about instead of Missouri."

"Look, I just want to sign."

"We could sign you, but I can give you only about $1,500."

"I'll take it!"

"Sorry, but I'm not going to send you out."

The next day coach Joe Slobko called me and said they'd love to have me at Garden City Community College. I was familiar with the program because Jamie Allison, who was from the Moline area, had gone to Garden City, and they were recruiting Dave Larson, a player from our rival high school. As it turned out, Dave and I both went to Garden City and became roommates.

Garden City was a great experience. We played more than 100 games a year for an intense, passionate coach. My first game playing there was in the fall against Colby

Community College. In the first inning I hit a double off the left-center-field wall and eventually came in to score. It was my first collegiate game—I was feeling pretty good. However, the leadoff batter in the bottom of the first grounded the ball to me...and I booted it. Joe Slobko wasn't happy. But what made it worse was that the runner scored. Joe started screaming, "That run's on you, Moore!" That was in the first inning of my first collegiate game. Joe didn't stop screaming at me all fall.

I called Dad during the fall and said, "This guy's crazy! I love his competitiveness, but he's on my case all the time."

My father's response isn't exactly what I wanted to hear. "Well, son, that means he cares. Your whole life you'll have someone telling you that you stink. You're going to stick it out at Garden City. We can readdress it at the end of the year." I decided to make it work.

You have to be prepared to fail in baseball, and Coach Slobko certainly prepared us for the mental side of the game. Slobko had a "boot camp" every January to get us into shape. The conditioning circuit was so intense that just the anticipation of it kept players awake at night.

As it turned out, playing for Joe was one of the best things that happened to me in my life. He was a rough, tough throwback, but an unbelievable competitor. I wanted to win for Joe because he cared so much about competing and winning. I loved playing for him.

I'll never forget during my sophomore year, we were having a good start to the season, including a top 20 ranking. Unfortunately, two of our better pitchers were suspended from the team. The night I found out, I was about to enter our dorm as Coach Slobko was walking out. I asked him what was going on, and he told me about the suspensions. "So you and the rest of your teammates are going to have to play better and I'm going to have to coach better." We went on to win 21 in a row before Barton County Community College broke the streak. We had the tying run on second with no outs but couldn't get him across. We ended the season with a 31–11 record.

Joe made us commit to doing our best. He'd fight anybody and never tolerated a lack of effort. There was no way to cut corners with Joe Slobko.

In addition to playing for Coach Slobko, another event changed my life during the time I was at Garden City. Although I originally gave my life to Christ in the third grade, I'm not sure I fully understood what that meant. My faith grew at Garden City as I participated in Bible studies with some of my teammates. I explored my walk in a deeper way before recommitting my life to Christ at that time.

GEORGE MASON

While I was at Garden City, my parents moved to Fairfax County, Virginia. So, after my two years of junior-college eligibility ended at Garden City, I headed east to play for coach Chuck Farris and the Reston Raiders in the Clark Griffith League, which was in the Washington, D.C., area.

That summer was memorable, mainly because of the baseball, but also because of one of my parents' neighbors. There was a girl across the street named Marianne Bixler, a student at Radford University, who was home visiting her parents for the summer. We didn't meet right away, though. I noticed her but I wasn't exactly what one might consider smooth when it came to girls. My smoothest move was making sure I went out for a jog when I knew

If I were scouting me as a player at George Mason University, out of the five tools, fielding and arm strength were my strongest attributes. *Photo courtesy of George Mason University Athletics*

she was out walking their dog. I later found out that the interest wasn't one-sided. She was keeping up with our Raiders team that summer. We "officially" met at the end of the summer and stayed in contact after she went back to school. It was a long-distance relationship for the most part. We were separated by about four hours during the school year, except when she'd come home for breaks. The next summer, in 1988, my parents had moved to Houston for another job opportunity, and I went to Toledo, Ohio, to play for a team in the Great Lakes Collegiate League, where one of my teammates was Dave Larson—my 1985 World Series traveling friend—who played at Indiana State after Garden City. With my parents in Texas, Marianne's visits home gave me a chance to spend a lot of time with her and her parents. Although we were dating, we weren't talking marriage yet because we each had other interests. For me, I wanted to continue the relationship with my first love: baseball.

Of course, most of my focus that first summer in Virginia was on playing for the Raiders and, I was hoping, finding my next college. The Clark Griffith League was perfect for that. It gave players with at least one year of eligibility remaining a chance to be seen by college coaches. One of the coaches I met was Billy Brown from nearby George Mason University. Billy was at our games recruiting one of my teammates. I was playing well enough, evidently, that he became interested in signing me, too.

I visited George Mason, which had a good baseball program. I liked the school, and it was going to be the most affordable place for me to go, so it was a perfect fit. That fit was tested, though, almost immediately.

Late that summer, the Raiders were playing in the Johnstown National Tournament, which was a huge amateur tournament. We were playing a team from Massachusetts, and I tore cartilage in my knee during a collision at home plate. The injury didn't require surgery, but I did have to go through rehab. I wasn't 100 percent yet when I showed up at George Mason. The school's athletic trainer wasn't going to release me to play, although I could practice. That's bad enough, but the NCAA at that time had placed a restriction on the number of fall games a team could play. So our fall schedule was already shorter, and now I'm being told that I can't play in games. I argued with the training staff, telling them that I was fine and should be able to play. They wouldn't budge, so Billy and I talked about it.

He wasn't budging, either. "The training staff doesn't want you to play, so you're not going to play. Just get the knee better."

"Look, I came here to play baseball," I told him. "If you don't play, me, I'm transferring. And by the way, I'm never going in the training room again."

Some people might think that sounds childish, but it was my intensity and passion for the sport talking. All I wanted to do was play baseball. As with a baseball game, every decision in life matters: who your friends are, where you work, lifestyle choices you make, whom you marry. Baseball was the constant thread for me during all of those decisions. Even on Friday and Saturday nights, I'd go hit instead of going out to parties. I'd blow off class to go hit if I could. I would've majored in baseball if the school offered it. I was obsessed with the sport. So, no, knowing how I felt, I was going to do everything possible to not let the training staff dictate whether I could play.

Looking back, if I had been Billy, I would've told me to hit the road. But Billy calmed me down and said, "Let me see what I can do."

When I saw him the next day, he told me, "If you think you can play, I'll trust you." That was a defining moment with Billy and me. If he was going to believe in me that quickly, it was going to be a positive experience for me. In turn, though, it made me more convinced to give him everything I had for the next two years — not that I wouldn't have given him 100 percent anyway. (And, no, I never did go back to the training room.)

On the field, Billy Brown was the ultimate field coordinator, running his program like a major league team. His practice schedules were some of the most detailed pieces of work you'd ever see, down to the minute. His budgets, I'd learn later, were down to the penny. He knew the game very well and because of that knowledge and the way he passed it down to us, he let his players play. He was very consistent with the way he did things, which is important over the course of a season.

Billy Brown, who'll be coaching his 35th season in 2015, prepared us for professional baseball. In addition to having more than 25 players drafted by major league teams, Billy's scouting and coaching tree has numerous branches.

On February 22, 2013, Billy Brown won his 900th career game with a victory over Wichita State.

COACH MOORE

If I were to put on my scouting hat and rate myself as a player, I'd say this of the five tools: below-average hitter, below-average power, average runner, above-average fielder, above-average arm. As a positional player, you have to be able to hit to stay in this game. Hitting right-handed without a lot of power and not being a plus-runner didn't bode well for me. At the time, while I was in college, I probably thought of myself as being a better player than I was. But I had a big heart to play. I can't look into anyone else's heart and say that mine was stronger, but I do know that I had an incredible desire to win and to do so with a team.

Right after my senior year, I wasn't drafted, so I started coaching third base for Chuck Farris with the Reston Raiders. Coach Farris was a pro and did things the right way. I was honored to get this opportunity. Late that fall, Billy Brown got a call from someone with the Erie Sailors of the independent New York–Penn League, inviting me to spring training. I worked out hard all winter in preparation for that opportunity.

Independent professional leagues are great because they offer more chances for players to get noticed. Baseball requires a lot of repetition and a lot of opportunities, and it's impossible to predict when a player will reach his ceiling. Several players who have started in independent leagues have ended up in the World Series. We actually have an independent team in the Kansas City area, the T-Bones. Throughout the years they've had players who, like me in 1989, are playing fresh out of college and looking for the opportunity to continue playing. And they've had former major league players. In fact, Ken Harvey and Joey Gathright are among former Royals who have played for the T-Bones, as has Alex Gordon's brother, Derek.

Playing independent baseball can help bring out a certain toughness and determination. A player has to have a great heart to play and compete, which is an important quality to being a successful baseball player. There are a lot of gifted players, and as one of my mentors, Jim Beauchamp, used to say, "Some are chosen." But it's your heart to play that fuels your passion and ultimately sustains you over the course of a baseball career. As your talent starts to deteriorate, this desire to win and passion to play is what helps players overcome the strains and the pains to keep pushing forward. Once you lose the toughness and passion to compete, it's tough to get them back. Longtime scout Jim Martz used to say, "Baseball is a tough game for tough people." In every baseball league on this planet from the little leagues to the major leagues, you must learn to manage failure well if you're going to be successful. That's life. There are very few nights when I put my head on my pillow and think, *Wow, everything went perfectly today.* It's a constant reminder that I must continue to develop my character, because the circumstances and events that take place daily in this game and in life will reveal your heart as a person.

o o o

Unfortunately, things didn't work out as I'd hoped with the Erie Sailors. They released me after two weeks. Before I left town, I called my father and said, "Well, Dad, it's over."

He replied, "Well, I'm sure they made a mistake. You'll probably get a call before you get to the airport." The call never came, but it's incredibly uplifting when someone believes in you and encourages you through the difficult times, as my father did that day.

I went back to George Mason, where Billy Brown gave me an opportunity to become his first paid graduate assistant. I jumped at the chance. Billy had me working with infielders, coaching first base, and recruiting. Eventually he let me coach third base. He showed a lot of trust in me and gave me a lot of responsibility, which made me a better baseball man.

One seed that Billy Brown planted that remains with me today is on the importance of pitching. Hitting takes care of itself, so pitching is key. Offensively, our goal was to make sure the opposing pitcher threw at least 15 pitches an inning. Essentially, we were scripting at-bats for most of our players. We left certain hitters alone, but we were always trying to get the starter out of the game by wearing him down. The game's evolved to where there are a lot of great arms in most teams' bullpens, but the pitching side has been crucial to me since working for Billy Brown. So, whether it's been at George Mason, Atlanta, or Kansas City, I always enjoy studying pitching and learning from men who are great at the craft.

o o o

To be the best I could be, I needed to coach in at least 100 games a year. The NCAA had restrictions on the number of games teams could play, so the only way to manage 100 in a season was to coach in the summer. Kevin Anderson, who was managing the Winchester Royals in the Valley Baseball League, which is a collegiate summer league, asked me to be his assistant. I accepted, but shortly after that, Kevin became the associate head coach at Eastern Carolina. His responsibilities there wouldn't allow him to coach in the summer, so they asked me to manage. At the time, Winchester was the premier franchise in the Valley

I always felt that when my playing career ended, I wanted become a coach. Billy Brown, my coach at George Mason, gave me that opportunity as his first paid graduate assistant.
Photo courtesy of George Mason University Athletics

League. The host family situation was excellent, travel was good, and the community embraced the team. I was fortunate to manage there. It taught me a lot, including how to deal with people.

During my first year, I was still an assistant at George Mason, so I would travel back and forth from Winchester to George Mason. With Winchester, the players would do their early work, and then we'd practice a fundamental as a team. One day I was going to be late getting there from George Mason, so I asked my assistant coach to run our bunt defense with the team. I got there earlier than I'd planned, and as I walked up to the field, I noticed we weren't running the bunt defense. I was furious. I fired the assistant coach on the spot without listening to any reason or excuse. Looking back on it, firing him was probably due to insecurity on my part. I've since learned that as a leader, your job is to help people get better and work together to find solutions. It's not about flipping the switch and moving on. Perhaps he had a valid reason for not working on the bunt defense at that time, but I didn't take time to listen. What he did was wrong, but I should've given him the opportunity work through that. Some people might be okay with my quick decision, but years later, I'm not.

Another important lesson I learned as a young coach was that you can push too hard. Some of my ex-players with Winchester constantly remind me of a time when we were in the midst of a five-game losing streak. We were playing in New Market, Virginia, and I wasn't satisfied with the effort of our players. When we returned to the stadium in the early morning hours, I ordered our assistant coach to turn on the stadium lights. I told the boys, "You have two choices. Pack your gear and go home or put your spikes on and let's go to work. However, if you choose the latter, you are telling me, your teammates, and yourself that you're committed to winning a championship here in Winchester." It was a risky proposition for me because there's a fine line between them focusing on the team or leaving. One of our better players, our shortstop Jason Cook, who went on to play for the Seattle Mariners and is now a players' agent, took a groundball off the lip during our late-night practice. He spent the next day in the dental chair and missed a few games. There was a renewed commitment, though, from the Winchester Royals, and we went on to win the Valley League championship.

I did things under Billy Brown's leadership that pushed the envelope, but Billy showed me grace and mercy. He could've fired me numerous times. He'd call me in from time to time and tell me to back off in certain areas. I've learned that if you want people to work for you and enjoy it, you need to give them some slack every once in a while.

When you're a young coach or GM, you have certain insecurities and you're learning how to deal with second-guessing and criticism. That goes back to biblical teaching. Tim Cash, my spiritual mentor, would say to me, "If you're motivated by praise, you're going to be defeated in criticism." That goes along with the quote by Warren Wiersbe, a well-known preacher and Christian writer, who said, "If praise humbles us, then criticism will build us up. But if praise inflates us, then criticism will crush us; and both responses lead to our defeat." Fighting that and finding the balance of being humbled by praise and not motivated by it is a daily process.

o o o

During the summer of 1991, about four years after Marianne and I first met, we had lightly discussed marriage, as couples who date for a few years tend to do. We went to a Fourth of July fireworks show at Herndon High School on a sweltering night. As we sat, waiting on the fireworks, we started talking about getting married. This time it was a little more serious. Although I loved her and could see us getting married, I wanted her to understand our future as well as I could explain it. "I'm not sure this is going to be the life you're going to want," I said. "I'm going to coach, and the lifestyle is very difficult. It's long hours, lots of travel. I could even get fired a time or two, which means we may have to relocate. But this is what I'm going to pursue. Oh, and by the way, I'm not going to make any money at all." I tried painting the clearest, most honest picture possible. Marianne understood all of that. At least she said she did. We became engaged later that summer and then got married on September 5, 1992.

Shortly after we got engaged, in my second year as a grad assistant, Flint Hill Academy in Virginia was starting a baseball program, and they offered me the head coaching position. On the surface, it seemed like a great situation. Since Marianne and I were about to be married, I thought, *Let's take this job and settle down in Northern Virginia.* Wanting to seek some counsel, I called Jim Moeller, who was a very successful coach at Fairfax High School. I coached Jim's son, Mark, in the Valley League. Jim, who had a John Wayne presence about him, would come to watch Mark, and I'd use the time to pick his brain as we chewed Lancaster (I've since quit chewing, by the way). We developed a good relationship, so I knew he'd be a good voice and would reaffirm my decision to go into high school coaching.

"Don't do it," he said. "As passionate as you are about the game, I don't think you'd be happy as a high school coach. Stay the course as a grad assistant, and future opportunities will come."

I was completely confused. I thought he'd give me validation, but it was just the opposite. The hardest thing to do as a young person is to trust people with experience. As a young player, it's tough to trust the process. Even now, as I'm knocking on the door of 50 years old, it's tough to trust the experience of others because we think we have all the answers. Every decision I've made, I've tried to seek counsel of someone with experience. Sure, I have core beliefs and values that ultimately guide me, but I like to get another perspective. For whatever reason, after hearing that from Jim, even though I thought I wanted the job at Flint Hill, I turned it down.

o o o

When I think about wise counsel — or just a person who was wise with experience — I think about former Negro Leagues star and Kansas City gem, Buck O'Neil.

I'd heard of Buck O'Neil over the years, but I'd never met him until 1994, when Ted Koppel was interviewing Buck on *Nightline*. It was during the time Ken Burns' *Baseball* documentary was airing on PBS. ABC used George Mason as the setting for Ted's interview with Buck. Since I was a baseball assistant coach, I got to meet both Ted and Buck. I just kept thinking how Buck was such an unbelievable ambassador for the game of baseball. His personality was so inviting, warm, and caring, and he had a special charisma. I've known only two other guys like that: Paul Snyder and Art Stewart.

When we came to Kansas City, one of the first public events I attended was the State Farm Legends Luncheon, which benefited the Negro Leagues Baseball Museum. Buck was always the emcee and star of that show. I wanted to attend those luncheons anytime I could, just to hear Buck's stories. At the first one, I reintroduced myself to Buck, who was very gracious and acted as if he remembered meeting me at George Mason. He definitely remembered doing the *Nightline* interview.

We all could learn countless lessons from Buck, led by his example of forgiveness. He also embraced every situation with a great, positive outlook. If we're breathing, there's a great plan for us. I didn't get a chance to know Buck as well as I would've liked, but I always took from him the wonderful example of taking a situation and making the best of it. All successful people I've met have that characteristic. Buck O'Neil certainly was a successful person.

o o o

While I was at George Mason, I had a couple opportunities to become a scout, but I wasn't interested because my focus was on coaching. Roy Clark, who was an area scout with the Atlanta Braves and someone who scouted George Mason and our Winchester Royals teams, called me one day late in 1994.

"Dayton, I'm about to become Atlanta's East Coast Scouting Supervisor, and I need to give the Braves three or four names of people who could take my place as an area scout," he said. "I'm going to give them only one name: yours."

"If I do it, I still want to be able to coach in the summer."

"That's not the position we have available."

"Thanks, but I'm not interested."

As far as I knew, that was the end of it. But a few days later, Roy called back.

"Just go down to Atlanta and meet with them," he insisted.

I didn't know Roy very well, but he was a great scout. He was an area scout for 12 years, and every year he signed at least one player who eventually became a major league player. An interesting side note to that, the first five years as an area scout he didn't get one player drafted. He signed players out of tryout camps. Roy Clark's commitment and pursuit of signing championship-caliber players was incredible. As I'd learn the second time he called me, he was a great salesman, too, partially due to his pushiness. I believe all good coaches and scouts are pushy.

Finally, I acquiesced and went down to Atlanta. I met with Scott Proefrock, who's currently an assistant general manager with Philadelphia; Don Mitchell, who became the first scouting director in Arizona Diamondbacks history; and assistant general manager for scouting and player development, Chuck LaMar, who went on to become the first general manager with the Tampa Bay Rays. Unfortunately, I didn't get a chance to work with these men very long, because all three left the following year for opportunities with other organizations. The interview obviously went well because they called back a few days later and offered me the job. I still wasn't convinced I wanted to go into scouting, but I decided to do it for at least four years and then get back into coaching.

Obviously, my career took a different path.

CHAPTER 3
A BRAVE NEW WORLD

IMAGINE YOU'RE A COLLEGE basketball coach from Lipscomb University, a relatively small, church-based school in Nashville, Tennessee, trying to recruit a four-star point guard from Ottawa, Kansas. You might be able to get an in-home visit with the young man, particularly if he has a Christian background. Otherwise, it might be a long shot. But then, imagine you're Bill Self, the head coach at the University of Kansas. Getting in front of that four-star point guard from Ottawa likely wouldn't be a problem given the Jayhawks' exposure and success.

Scouting and signing baseball players is a lot like recruiting. And, in the baseball world in 1994, particularly in the Southeast, the Atlanta Braves were the Kansas Jayhawks. Most of their games were on TBS at the time, and they were early in their run of 14-straight division titles. As a scout for the Atlanta Braves at that time, every young player invited you into his house, and every coach rolled out the red carpet for you. In the same way a high school basketball player in the Midwest would love to tell his buddies that Bill Self was sitting at his family's dinner table talking about KU, every aspiring baseball player in the Southeast would love to brag to his friends that a scout from the Atlanta Braves was sitting at his family's dinner table.

We didn't have that when we came to Kansas City in 2006; in fact, it was the opposite. We were fighting for credibility. We had to change the perception. That perception was already incredibly strong with the Braves when I started as the area scouting supervisor for the mid-Atlantic states during baseball's work stoppage in 1994. Stan Kasten, John Schuerholz, Bobby Cox, Paul Snyder, and other scouts and player development people did that heavy lifting for the organization a few years earlier. I was injected into the middle of that.

What a learning experience! As a young scout I couldn't have picked better mentors in the business than men such as Paul, Roy Clark, Donnie Williams, Bill Fischer, Jose Martinez, Jim Beauchamp, and Bill Lajoie. These gifted baseball people took time to pour into me all that they could about scouting and player develop ment. During spring training we spent a lot of hours on the golf cart, watching players and discussing the game. And then we burned the midnight oil every night, as we talked about players, or they swapped stories from their illustrious baseball careers. I was entranced as I soaked up all that I could.

As an area scouting supervisor, my job was to put the Braves in a position to draft and sign the top players throughout the mid-Atlantic region. It was my job to know everything possible about the top players in the area—knowing their strengths and weaknesses on the field, of course, but most importantly their makeup, and their family. I'd then report back to my regional supervisor and national supervisor, so they could filter the information to the scouting director. Really, the area scouting supervisor is the backbone of a team's amateur scouting staff.

I had a good feel for the overall job from my time as the recruiting coordinator at George Mason, which also helped because I knew the college and high school coaches in the region, plus many of the scouts from other organizations. Of course, professional scouting is a little different from college recruiting because you're "putting a dŏllar sign on the muscle." That adds considerable pressure to the job.

My first draft with the Braves was in June 1995. The club selected two players from my region in the first 10 rounds: power-hitting first baseman Jimmy Scharrer in the second round and shortstop Jerry Vecchioni in the seventh round. Both players were in high school. Jimmy was from Cathedral Prep in Erie, Pennsylvania, and Jerry was from Patapsco High in Dundalk, Maryland. They both had a lot of talent, even though neither player made it to the major leagues. Jimmy had great power, great makeup, but he couldn't cover the holes in the strike zone. He was a very intelligent kid with a great family. Although Jimmy had scholarship offers to play football and baseball, he signed with us for a $250,000 signing bonus. Jimmy spent six years in our system, maxing out at Double A, before becoming a linebacker at Duke University.

Jerry had a lot of talent but couldn't get his priorities straight off the field. He played two years in our minor league system before the Braves had enough and released him. It still bothers me to this day that I missed so badly on this player.

Again, though, as a baseball scout you're paid for your opinion and expected to get it right, so there's no excuse for getting it wrong.

"My" first player to make it to the major leagues was Mark DeRosa. The Braves took him in the seventh round of the 1996 MLB Amateur Draft out of the University of Pennsylvania. He was a shortstop and starting quarterback at Penn, so he had strength, athleticism, high intelligence, and a great competitive spirit. He exemplified winning, which was the biggest attribute I saw in him. He fulfilled those expectations and beyond. Mark played 16 years in the major leagues—seven of those with Atlanta. A highlight for me was seeing Mark in the starting lineup for the visiting Texas Rangers in my first game as general manager for the Royals. DeRo retired after the 2013 season and is now a terrific analyst on MLB Network. Because of his duties with the network, we were able to spend time together during the 2014 World Series.

The toughest part of scouting for me was striking a proper balance between the demands of the job and my personal life. By nature, successful scouts are driven and competitive, and the job calls for you to be on the road constantly. After all, you're going against the best evaluators in the world who are working for 29 other clubs. The work is endless; you can always do more. You can always drive 200 more miles to see a player. You can always set up another workout. You can always make another phone call to a player or a coach. So managing the time with a personal life, especially a young family, as was my case, is challenging. It's important to nurture a young family so it'll turn into a great family. That was stressful, but Marianne was, is, and always will be a tremendous supporter. Her support, encouragement, and strong faith are a few of the reasons I've admired her for my entire adult life. But Paul Snyder, the Braves scouting director when I was first hired, used to say, "Your wife deserves to know where you're putting your head down at night. Whenever she wants you home, you drop what you're doing and you go home." There have been only a couple of times when Marianne has said, "Dayton, you need to come home." And, because of Paul's sage advice, I've done just that.

Besides life lessons about being a better husband and father, Paul taught me by example about humility and forgiveness. When John Schuerholz left Kansas City for Atlanta, he hired Chuck LaMar and moved Paul out of the role of scouting director. Paul likely had his personal moments of anger or frustration, but he never complained or bad-mouthed anybody. He embraced his new role and continued to work with a great smile on his face, with as much enthusiasm as he ever had to make the Braves better. Because of the way Paul handled that situation, when Chuck, one of the men who interviewed me when I was first hired as a scout, left to become the first general manager at Tampa Bay, Paul was a natural choice to oversee scouting and player development again. If he had handled the situation in a negative way and burned that bridge with John, he wouldn't have had the opportunity to return to that leadership role. Instead, he handled the reassignment with grace and class. The entire organization was happy that Paul was back in that role.

MOVING TO ATLANTA

After two years as an area scouting supervisor, Paul called and said that they wanted me to move to Atlanta to be a part of the front office as a baseball operations assistant. I was comfortable and happy working as a scout.

"Paul, I'm not sure this works for us," I told him. "I'm not sure I want to be in the front office."

A few minutes after we hung up, I got a call from Roy Clark. "Have you lost your mind?" he asked. "Are you crazy? You have a chance to be around John Schuerholz, Paul Snyder, and Bobby Cox."

I thought a little more about the opportunity in Atlanta after talking with Roy, and the positives seemed to outweigh the negatives. Our first child, daughter Ashley, had been born in January 1996. Marianne and I decided when we got married that, in a life centered on God and family, we wanted her home once we had children. Making $27,000 as a scout, living in a $150,000 townhouse in the Washington, D.C., area required two incomes.

As we looked further into the possibility of going to Atlanta, my salary was going to increase by $5,000, which wasn't huge, but the cost of living in Atlanta was less than D.C., so it would allow Marianne to stay home with Ashley. The decision was still difficult because Marianne was born and raised in northern Virginia, and her parents still lived in the area. But after discussing it more and praying about it, we decided that professionally it was a win and personally it was a win.

> I was going to bring someone into the office in Atlanta. I told John Schuerholz that I thought I would bring Dayton Moore in. He said, "Holy cow, Paul, he's only scouted for two years." I said, "John, you were a schoolteacher. Did any of your students ever skip a grade? This young man has skipped a couple grades." He came in and was a dish rag—he sopped up as much knowledge as he could.
>
> —Paul Snyder

o o o

Basically, the baseball operations assistant is a catchall position with exposure to multiple departments because you're at everyone's disposal. It was a chance to learn a different side of the organization. Occasionally, John would call me in for a project. Job title aside, based on his presence, expectations for the organization, professionalism, and class, if John asked us to do something, we did it without hesitation.

The baseball operations department in Atlanta was very much scouting and player-development driven because of John. To this day, he is a big believer in scouts and minor league managers and coaches. He understands they're the most important part of the organization. The area scout puts you in a position to select and sign the best players from his territory, and then, as

Hall of Fame scout Paul Snyder and his wife, Petie, came to Kansas City for the first two games of the 2014 World Series. Paul taught me so many lessons about this business and about life while I worked with him in Atlanta. *Photo courtesy of Dayton Moore*

a general manager, you have to trust the scout's vision of that player. Once the player is signed, it's up to the minor league manager and coaches to create the atmosphere and the attitude that foster the player's desire to compete. Basically, the coach is developing the scout's vision of the player.

As he did in Kansas City, John used the farm system well in Atlanta, but that's not the only reason his teams have been successful. Kansas City and Atlanta were successful under John Schuerholz because of his great spirit to compete. Sure, he's hired good people and allowed them to do their jobs, but he does all he can to win each and every year.

o o o

One great advantage to being in Atlanta was spending time with Paul Snyder. I would try to beat him to the office every morning—which was tough because Paul arrived earlier than most people—and then I'd go into his office with my coffee, while he drank his Diet Coke, and I'd learn as much as I could from him. We would discuss and break down players from all different eras, and he would talk about great scouts such as Bill White and Fred Shaffer, and some of his mentors, such as John Mullen, Bill Lucas, and Roland Hemond. Paul taught me how to ask good questions and then to listen. He'd always try to spend time with the area scouts in their territory, going over their draft list during one-on-one conversations. Paul stressed that scouts should stay aggressive when making player recommendations.

"If you're not making mistakes," he'd say, "you're not aggressive enough. This gets harder and harder. A lot of scouts tend to back off later in their careers because they failed so much along the way."

Paul was exactly right. Everyone in this game makes their share of mistakes to justify being fired, but think about this: if you turn in 100 players on your draft list and 15 make it to the major leagues, that's outstanding. You failed with 85 percent of the names, but that 15 percent makes it successful. The 85 percent gives you room to learn from your mistakes.

> *The conversations Dayton and I had in the mornings were similar to what Bobby Cox and I did when he first became general manager in Atlanta. We would meet in his office at 5:30 every morning. He was drinking black coffee, and I'd drink Diet Coke, and we'd talk baseball. Dayton was the same. He was a really impressionable and impressive young man. If anything surprised me about him it's how fast he grasped everything.*
>
> *—Paul Snyder*

Paul, who suffered a stroke in the mid-1970s when he was 40 and had to relearn how to write, is an amazing person. He has one of the warmest and most inviting personalities you can imagine, with a great presence and a lot of energy. You'd want anyone you know and care about to meet Paul Snyder.

o o o

Although John Schuerholz was the general manager who turned the Braves into a dynasty, Paul Snyder's draft picks before John got there helped lay the foundation for a world championship team.

Throughout most of the 1970s and '80s, the Atlanta Braves were one of the worst teams in baseball. From 1970 until John became their general manager in 1990, the Braves won the division one time (1982) and finished next-to-last or last 13 times. Shortly before John took over, president Stan Kasten and general manager Bobby Cox, along with Paul and his scouts, were loading up the organization with minor league talent. Six of the eight players in the 1995 lineup that won the World Series were drafted or signed as amateur free agents from 1983 to 1990: Javy Lopez, Mark Lemke, Jeff Blauser, Chipper Jones, Ryan Klesko, and David Justice. Those young players were in place when John arrived, but as Paul often said, John brought a competitive edge and taught the Braves how to win.

As a player, Paul came up through the Braves' organization as a first baseman and outfielder, but through his experience and observations during a lifetime in the game, Paul was very astute in evaluating pitchers, as proven by some of the pitchers the Braves signed and developed on his watch: Steve Avery, Mark Wohlers, and Tom Glavine, to name a few. Once those pitchers developed, they played in Atlanta for Bobby Cox, who was another keen pitching evaluator.

I noticed in spring training every year, Bobby would be sitting in the bullpen while other drills were going on around the field. One time I asked him why he spent so much time in the bullpen. He said, "Because these guys, these pitchers, are the most important part of our team. This is an area you have to manage well."

I'd start to watch from a distance, but Bobby inevitably would invite me to watch with him as Glavine, Greg Maddux, and John Smoltz threw a side session. Watching those three throw a side session was the most intense thing

I've seen in baseball. They were so focused and dialed in to what they were doing. I was afraid to breathe because I didn't want to disrupt their rhythm. They were trying to deliver each baseball to the catcher's mitt with complete perfection. Every time they threw a baseball, even when playing catch in the outfield, it was with a purpose. They tried to execute a perfect throw every time they threw a baseball. That focus, discipline, dedication to the small details, and precision is why they're Hall of Famers.

Bobby knew how to handle pitching as well as any manager I've seen. He knew when he could push those guys and when to get them out of the game. He had a great relationship with his pitching staff and always had their back.

THE "BRAVES WAY"

Bobby Cox had a strong belief in his players, but players throughout the entire organization learned they'd have to play a certain way—the "Braves Way"—if they wanted to play for Bobby. That meant selfless baseball with a strong desire to compete. It meant pitchers had to throw strikes. It meant position players had to play solid defense. When I was the farm director, we told players, "You won't be able to play like that for No. 6." That applied to all facets of being a professional baseball player. If a player didn't conduct himself in a professional way, Bobby wouldn't want him in the clubhouse.

I remember when one of our top prospects, who's a major league player today with another organization, was in High A ball, we sent him to play center field in a major league spring training game. During batting practice, he was in center field, dancing around to the music. Bobby saw that and told me later that night, "Hey, don't send that guy over here anymore. If he's going to be dancing like that in pregame, he doesn't need to be here."

Bobby was a no-nonsense manager who loved his players and was loved by them. My first experience with Bobby's belief in his players was in 2000, the year after we lost shortstop Walt Weiss. Our top position player in the system was shortstop Rafael Furcal, who had finished the '99 season in High A Myrtle Beach after spending most of it in Class A Macon. Although we thought highly of Raffy, I was apprehensive to recommend him to Bobby as the Braves starting shortstop because in '99 he committed 34 errors between the two Class A stops. With the Atlanta pitching staff, Furcal was going to have to play relatively error-free at shortstop. Many of us felt it would be better to have Furcal start the 2000 season in Double A to work on his defense—it certainly didn't appear as though he was ready to skip both Double A and Triple A. When we talked to Bobby about our options and how most people didn't feel Raffy was ready for the major leagues, Bobby said, "Ah, he'll be fine. He'll do well." Bobby firmly believed in Furcal because he knew Raffy had talent and he knew that Raffy believed in himself. Bobby was right. Rafael Furcal went on to win the Rookie of the Year award in 2000.

A few years later, in 2005, Kelly Johnson, one of the Braves' supplemental first-round draft picks in 2000, had just broken into the major leagues. He was a great kid and a promising young hitter, but he was a perfectionist and incredibly hard on himself. He was struggling shortly after he got called up, so Jim Beauchamp and I went to the clubhouse to see Kelly and encourage him. We could tell he was dejected. Beech and I went into Bobby's office, and I said, "Bobby, Kelly is really down on himself. Do you think we need to send him to the minor leagues?"

"Heck, no! I have him hitting in the three-hole tonight. He has a great swing and he's going to be just fine. He's going to be more than fine." It reinforced the belief Bobby had in his players. Breaking into the major leagues is never easy, especially on a team that's expected to be in the World Series as the Braves were at the time, but Bobby helped eliminate as much pressure as he could from the young players.

Like John Schuerholz, Bobby always trusted his players and our scouting and player development departments.

o o o

In January 2004 we had a workout for a 16-year-old named Elvis Andrus, who was a top player in Venezuela. It was rumored that the Yankees had a deal done with him, but since it was only a rumor, we worked him out. The early signing period for international players begins on July 2. That day came and went without Elvis signing with anyone, so we continued to work him out, but we couldn't get him signed.

We were going to be back in Venezuela in January 2005 for a workout with various players. Elvis, who was invited, had been in the Dominican Republic, working out for the Texas Rangers. Allegedly, the Rangers had their owners and top baseball executives there to see Elvis. None of us knew how much money he wanted for signing, but we had $325,000 on the table. Texas, it was rumored, offered him $350,000.

Our workout in Venezuela on that January morning was scheduled to start at 9:00. When the tryout began at

9:00, Elvis was nowhere to be seen. We figured immediately that we'd lost him. Suddenly, at 9:15, he showed up. He quickly got loose and blended in with the other kids in the workout. He got in the batting cage and started roping opposite-field line drives. And then he took some reps at shortstop, even though there was some question whether that was the best position for him. It didn't matter because his bat was good enough to put him at second or third if we needed to. As we watched the workout, I turned to J.J. Picollo, who was Atlanta's assistant director of player development at the time, and said, "We have to get this kid signed."

Afterward I asked Elvis and his agent what it would take. "Five hundred thousand dollars," they said. I told them we had a deal, and we shook hands.

We knew Elvis was a future major league player. His makeup was strong, he was intelligent, and he wanted to play. We were confident enough in his ability that a $500,000 signing bonus was a small ingredient in the grand scheme of him becoming a major league player. We weren't going to haggle. We had to make a decision then because we couldn't wait and possibly lose him. He signed on January 25, 2005. Ironically, in 2007, Elvis was part of a seven-player trade between Atlanta and Texas that included Mark Teixeira going to the Braves. Elvis reached the majors with the Rangers in 2009 and emerged as one of the top shortstops in the American League.

As long as we had the money in the budget to sign Elvis, John Schuerholz was supportive and gave us the freedom to do that. Frankly, John's two main questions whenever we were evaluating or attempting to sign a high-profile player were: 1) is the player worth the money? and

2) do we have it in the budget? If the answer to both of those was yes, then we knew we had the green light.

That doesn't mean things always worked out. We had pitcher Felix Hernandez working out at our complex at Disney World in Florida. Felix was 16, but he already had the makings of a special pitcher. His delivery was consistent and he had command of his breaking ball with power. We knew that several teams were very interested, including the Yankees, Red Sox, and Mariners. I called John and said, "I'm looking at a really good pitcher whom I think we should sign."

"How much will it cost us?"

"I'd say $800,000 or possibly $900,000."

"Is he worth it?"

The answer was yes, and we could afford it, but we offered Felix $750,000. We had more money in the budget but tried to sign him for less. As it turned out, he signed with Seattle for a reported $710,000.

MORE LESSONS LEARNED

Of course, when you're in a winning environment, as we were experiencing in Atlanta, you're bound to meet people who offer great life and baseball lessons. As I mentioned earlier in the chapter, most of those lessons came from my main mentors with the Braves. But I learned other terrific lessons along the way.

Hall of Fame pitcher Phil Niekro was one of those teachers. Phil, who loves to share stories, came to spring training every year. We were talking one day about success and failure in baseball. He said, "When I learned to accept losing without being defeated, my career took off." In other words, you have to learn from your mistakes and improve. A lot of negative things happen during a game, not to mention an entire season. People from the outside can look at those failures and pile on the player, so he has to be tough and continue to move forward in a passionate, disciplined way.

o o o

Jeff Blauser was a baseball player. He was no-nonsense, 100 percent about winning. Bobby Cox told us one time, "You gotta get players with tools, but don't forget about the Mark Lemkes and Jeff Blausers of the world, because you win championships with players like them." Jim Beauchamp kept telling me that we needed to get Blauser, who was retired from playing, back in the organization. So I met with Blaus to talk about how we could use him to teach baseball and grow a new generation of players. In my mind, he was the perfect person to do that. He was dedicated and loyal to the Braves, and he had a heart to do it right. That's what allows you to be successful — undying belief and discipline to persevere. Blauser exemplified that. Commitment and talent have nothing to do with each other. You can have a lot of talent, but if you're not committed, you're not going to reach your ceiling. Blauser's commitment to win is what made him a player. He didn't have the tools of Furcal, Andruw Jones, or Chipper Jones, but his commitment to be the best, learn the game, and beat you with his mind, is what made him stand out. It's important to get those people in the organization. Blaus was a roving instructor for three years before taking over as manager for a year at Double A Mississippi. After traveling and sacrificing for a lot of years, Jeff is now enjoying life at home.

[Dayton and I] had crossed paths when I was playing, but he was scouting and didn't have an active role. I really got to know him when I came back. I told Dayton that, if it weren't for him, I don't know that I would've taken the position when I did. I don't know that I would've come back right then, but I was a big believer in what he was trying to do. Not only did I want to work for the Atlanta Braves organization, but I also wanted to work for Dayton Moore. I wanted to see him accomplish what he set out to do, and I was excited to get the opportunity to learn from him and help him along the way.

— *Jeff Blauser*

OTHER OPPORTUNITIES

I've never pursued other positions. I've never sought a job in this game. Most of the time in Atlanta, it was John Schuerholz telling me, "This is what we need you to do," and I did it. That resulted in me going from baseball operations assistant to assistant director of scouting to director of international pro scouting to director of player personnel to assistant general manager (although that was more of a title because my job didn't change much).

During the 2005 general managers' meetings, John told me that Larry Lucchino, president of the Boston Red Sox, wanted to interview me for their general manager's job. Theo Epstein had helped put together the Red Sox club that won the 2004 World Series, but then he resigned after the '05 season.

I told John I wasn't interested in interviewing.

"They're in our hotel; just go meet with them," he said.

Anytime someone is interested in having you interview for a job, it's both flattering and humbling. That certainly was the case with the Red Sox, but going into it I didn't feel, personally and professionally, that I wanted to pursue that job. My heart has to be locked in to get a job done, and I didn't feel a pull for Boston.

Still, I met with Larry and team chairman Tom Werner. We had a good meeting, and the thought of being the GM of the Red Sox might've been tempting for a brief moment. Ultimately, the timing wasn't right. Personally, our kids were nine, six, and three at the time, and Atlanta was home. Professionally, the Red Sox had accomplished the greatest thing in baseball by winning the World Series a year earlier, snapping their 86-year championship drought. I've been asked if the rumors of Theo's strained working relationship with Larry had anything to do with my decision, and the answer is no. I never judge a situation based on someone else's experience, because every situation is different. I can't look at life through anyone else's eyes. I can't speak to Theo's relationship because I wasn't there. It was a timing issue for me.

About a week after meeting with them, I called Larry to withdraw my name from consideration. Those conversations are never easy, but you have to be up-front and very transparent. It was humbling that they considered me.

There were two other times that John told me about teams wanting to interview me to become their next general manager: Arizona and Cincinnati. The Diamondbacks were close to completing their interviews when John said they wanted to meet with me. I told him I wasn't interested. And then the Reds job came open and they called John to see if I was interested. Again, I said no.

It would have to be the perfect situation for me to leave Atlanta.

CHAPTER 4
"YOU CAN'T WIN IN KANSAS CITY"

I NEVER WANTED TO BE the general manager of a major league baseball team. That wasn't my goal in life. That's not why I didn't pursue jobs in Arizona, Boston, or Cincinnati while I was working for Atlanta. It's simply that my father taught me to work every job like it would be the last one I'd ever have. It's just a matter of being content and giving your current employer the best you have each and every day. Baseball is very competitive, and it requires a high level of focus each and every day if you're going to be successful. There is no time to think about your future.

Rumors flew around that Royals general manager Allard Baird was going to be let go. I didn't ponder the Kansas City job at all or hope that they would call me. (Besides, as my wife, Marianne, would say, I'm usually the last to know.) My focus at the time—as it always has been and always will be—was on my current team. So in May 2006, I didn't think twice about it when John Schuerholz asked me to lunch, as he did from time to time. With the amateur draft about a month away, that easily could've been our topic of conversation. But as we sat down to eat inside a restaurant at the CNN Center, John's main point wasn't to discuss the Braves.

"The Royals are looking for a new general manager," he said. "David and Dan Glass are going to be in Atlanta, and they'd like to meet with you."

Even though Kansas City was off to a bad start and had lost 100 games three times in four years, my interest was piqued more than it had been for any other general manager's position. Growing up, the Royals were *my* team. Even as I was working for the Braves, that boyhood love continued. I followed them more than any team in the American League and probably as much as I followed any team, besides our opponents in the National League East.

That's not to say I was reading every article I could find or reading Kansas City's box scores daily, as I'd done with my grandmother in Coldwater, Kansas, but I still considered myself a fan. In 2004 George Brett came to Atlanta for a MasterCard commercial. John, knowing I was a Royals fan growing up, introduced us. George was very gracious and kind. We talked a little about his playing days, and then he talked a little about the Royals' struggles. After that conversation I followed the Royals a little more, but that's not to say I kept close track of the club.

I knew they'd been struggling—they likely wouldn't be looking for a general manager if times were great—but there's an initial interest when your boyhood team, the one with which you share an emotional attachment, wants to talk with you about a job.

"Look," said John, who was the Royals' general manager before joining the Braves, "I think you should at least talk with them."

My mind was already made up. I was going to meet with the Kansas City Royals.

It was going to be tough for me to see Dayton go, but you could tell he was a rising star. That came from not only in his ability, but also his persona—his character. He's a man of integrity and he treated people that way. You knew he was going to be a success and do well. People will find reasons to go to work for a guy like that.

—John Schuerholz

Later that day I told Marianne about it. As always, she was very supportive. Deep down she didn't think we'd leave Atlanta then or, perhaps, ever.

A few days later I met Royals owner David Glass and his son, team president Dan Glass, for the first time at the DeKalb-Peachtree Airport, one of the smaller airports in the Atlanta area. It was obvious that Mr. Glass (David) was very frustrated with the Royals' lack of progress as an organization. He indicated they wanted to build a model organization through scouting and player development that would stand the test of time. He was willing to commit the necessary resources to build an organization from the ground up. "We need someone with fresh ideas and a fresh battle plan," he said. "I don't want to be embarrassed at the major league level, but I don't want to sacrifice the minor leagues for the sake of the major league team."

Mr. Glass and Dan's directive was very clear: they expected a major league team that reflected homegrown talent. We all agreed that to commit to this process would take a lot of time.

The initial meeting with Mr. Glass and Dan ended with handshakes and the promise that they'd be back in touch after they talked with other potential candidates. Whether it was because of or in spite of the challenge the job would present, I was now more interested in joining the Kansas City Royals than I was Boston or any other club.

> *Dayton was our first choice and the only guy we really wanted. I've been around baseball since the mid-1940s, so I knew quite a few people who have been around awhile. I called some of them and asked who'd be the best candidate who isn't presently a general manager. The only name I got was Dayton's. One huge proponent was John Hart, whom I've known since his early days in Cleveland, and I've come to really value his opinion over the years. He was strong on his opinion that Dayton was the best candidate out there. Dayton is the classification that I call a "baseball lifer." These guys have been around the game all their lives, they love the game, and they have an appreciation for it. Dayton had a reputation of being a great judge of talent. So I called John Schuerholz and said, "John, I'd like to interview Dayton." He gave us his blessing, so I called Dayton and arranged a time for Dan and me to fly to Atlanta and meet with him. When we got together, we told him what we wanted to do, what our plan was, and how we proposed going about it. It was obvious that Dayton and I have a lot in common. He believes strongly that players need ability, of course, but they need to have character and integrity and fit in the organization. He's also a really intense kid who's as obsessed with winning—and winning the right way—as I am. I loved that character matters nearly as much as the physical ability to him.*
>
> *—David Glass*

True to their word, they called back a few days later and offered me the job. I hadn't done much research because the June amateur draft was approaching quickly, so I asked if I could have some time to think about it.

I did as much research as I could on the players, the farm system, their processes, and development to try to fully grasp what the challenge would be. Perhaps because of the comfort in Atlanta or the upcoming draft, I had one foot in and one foot out. I wasn't expecting to leave, so I wasn't doing a ton of research.

Most of my research, as I've done throughout my life with any big decision, was seeking wise counsel. In this case, I spoke with Atlanta confidants, such as John Schuerholz, Paul Snyder, and Roy Clark, as well as many people around the game who were either close to the situation in Kansas City or aware of similar situations. The overwhelming majority of the people I spoke with advised against taking the job. Want to know some of the things I heard?

Don't take the job. You can't win in Kansas City.

I wouldn't do it; it's a professional graveyard.

Because of the economics of today's game, you can't win quickly enough. The fans are great, but they're tired of waiting. You'll be fired before you have a chance to succeed.

There's very little talent in the farm system. The market is not going to allow you to spend money on free agency, and you'll have to overspend in the draft. Plus they don't have an international program.

You'd be foolish to go to Kansas City when you might have an opportunity for the same job in Atlanta.

With all of the negative talk surrounding the job and the organization, it was a difficult struggle. Unfortunately, wrestling with the decision turned unwittingly into a great weight-loss plan. Up to that point, it was the most stressful few weeks in my 39 years on this earth.

"YOU CAN'T WIN IN KANSAS CITY"

I thought Dayton could be successful in Kansas City. That job needed someone with a background in either scouting or player development, and Dayton had skills in both of those areas. He knew what had to be done and he was going to carry that out. My concern and some of my last words to him before he took the job: "Be sure your owner understands and believes in what you're going to do." The Glass family appears to have believed in Dayton's plan.

—Paul Snyder

Out of everyone besides Marianne, I probably talked with John the most about the decision, and he was very supportive. On the morning I was going to call Mr. Glass to give him my decision, I met once more with John. He didn't talk me out of it, but when I left his office, I called Marianne and told her, "I'm not taking the job. We're staying here."

I loved working for John, with our entire scouting and player development department, and, of course, manager Bobby Cox, and our players. The Royals were my boyhood team, but Atlanta was home. Our family was thriving in Atlanta. The girls were doing well in school (Robert hadn't started yet), and we had a wonderful church family. I was traveling quite a bit, but Marianne had a great support system with our close group of friends. The reasons to stay far outweighed the reasons to go.

After I called Marianne and told her we were staying in Atlanta, I felt a sense of relief as did she. However, as the day went on, I wasn't at peace. I knew we were playing it safe. Looking for one more opinion, I called Tim Cash, who is one of my spiritual mentors. We worked through the positives and negatives.

"What are you afraid of?" he asked. "Why are you playing it safe?"

I told him, "I'm not John Schuerholz. I don't have his skill set. Nobody can duplicate what John has done. I've always been a scout and development guy. At my roots, I'm just a fungo-hitting baseball kid."

Tim laughed and said, "Don't worry about doing it like John Schuerholz. You need to do it your way. You can go there and build something special." And then he added, "God gave you your own skills and talents. You need to trust God."

If I was to be gut-level honest with myself, I was confronting a fear of the unknown that we all face with life-changing decisions. We were very comfortable in Atlanta. I was afraid to live 2 Timothy 1:7, where we're told, "For God did not give us a Spirit of fear but of power and love and self-control."

My relationship with God was huge throughout this decision. Prayer has always been a big part of my life. When I have decisions to make or big upcoming meetings, I pray. I knew that turning this decision over to God was important, which can be easier said than done.

I'm not going to say that God spoke to me and told me to take the Kansas City job. It might happen that way for some people, but that's not what happened for me. Praying for guidance and wisdom in a decision doesn't mean we're guaranteed to make the right one. I'm a big believer that where you are in life is where God wants you to be. One of my arguments with myself was that there would be plenty of good work to do in Atlanta just like there would be in Kansas City.

After talking with Tim Cash and praying more for guidance, I started to have this internal conversation:

Why did you get into athletics?
The competition and the challenge.
Well, wouldn't it be fun to build something special in Kansas City? It may not work out the way you want, and it may not have a happy ending. But go challenge yourself and build a culture.

That was it. I had unbelievable mentors and support in a terrific learning environment in Atlanta. For those men and all that they'd taught me, I needed to go and prove that we could do something special. The challenge of building in Boston wouldn't have been there because the Red Sox already won the World Series, Arizona won it a few years earlier, and Cincinnati was a postseason-caliber team. Kansas City would give me a great proving ground and, by being successful, honor men such as Paul Snyder, Roy Clark, and John Schuerholz.

On May 30, I called Mr. Glass and accepted the position. Kansas City, Kansas City, here we come.

It was funny, after Dayton told John Schuerholz he was coming to Kansas City, John good-naturedly got on my case. He called and said, "Look, I told you to talk to him, not hire him!" John is a big admirer of Dayton, as well. They had a good relationship. John had a great run in Kansas City, of course, so we all get along great.

—David Glass

This seems like the perfect time to put to rest a rumor about my discussions with Mr. Glass and Dan. Many Royals fans have believed that Dan, as team president, interfered with Allard Baird on occasion. I can't speak to whether that's true, but it's been reported over the years that I demanded total autonomy over baseball operations,

Royals owner David Glass (right) and his son, team president Dan Glass, have been incredibly supportive and patient since we arrived in Kansas City in June 2006.

without any input from Dan, before I'd take the job. That's simply not true. Again, I can't speak for Allard's situation because I wasn't here and I didn't research his relationships with people throughout the organization, but there has not been a single time when Dan has interfered in any way, shape, or form. In fact, Dan and Mr. Glass have been extremely supportive. Mr. Glass is not only one of the most successful businessmen in the history of our country, he's an incredible owner and wants what's best for Kansas City and the Royals.

> *No, Dayton didn't have any demands, and there's really no basis for saying that he did. As far as Dan, he and Dayton developed a good relationship immediately.*
>
> —*David Glass*

For the first time in a month, once I called Mr. Glass to accept the job, I had some peace. That's not to say it was easy to leave Atlanta. On the contrary, breaking away was hard. I don't know if I spoke to every scout, manager, coach, trainer, and clubhouse person in the Atlanta system, but I had emotional conversations with many of them. I had developed close friendships during a dozen years with all of them.

> *I'm not surprised he took the Kansas City job over Boston and other possible opportunities. He and I had conversations during all of those contemplations, but it was always his instincts, his beliefs, and his family's feelings that he took into consideration. I felt that Kansas City was the perfect place for him to go. It was an organization that hadn't enjoyed success a lot in a very long time, so they were ripe for new leadership, ripe for a new program, and ripe for a new Royals Way to get it done. I thought he was the perfect guy going into the perfect place.*
>
> *—John Schuerholz*

One of the best conversations was with manager Bobby Cox. We were in his office, and Bobby, being the encourager and supporter that he is, talked to me about the general manager–manager relationship (remember, he'd been a GM, also). One thing he said that I'll never forget: "It's a very important relationship, but just be you." Think of all the times life would be easier if we did that: "just be you."

Bobby's words reminded me of the Bible's David and Goliath story. Most of the time our focus in that story is on the seemingly overmatched David taking down the giant Goliath with his sling and a stone. But one part of that story that sometimes gets overlooked is when David said he'd take on Goliath, Saul put his coat of armor and helmet on David. In case you're not familiar with the story, David is a shepherd and, from what we understand, basically a teenaged boy who isn't very big. So, after he tries to walk around for a minute in Saul's armor, he takes it off and says it's not him; he's not used to the armor. Instead, he just grabbed his staff, five stones, and his sling. David needed to face Goliath his own way. In much the same way, if I was going to have any success in Kansas City, I needed to trust God and use the gifts He's given me to lead.

That's the way Bobby Cox managed—as his own person, in his own style. I have a strong appreciation for Bobby and his coaching staff, winning the division for 14 years under a pretty big microscope. I don't think there's another profession that requires you to meet with the media twice a day, but win or lose, Bobby always handled that with terrific grace. He stressed to our scouting and player development departments that it was more important to get him the right players, which didn't always mean the most talented players. "Just give us players that know how to play and love to win, and we'll make it work." There's a lot of Bobby Cox in Ned Yost. I didn't know Ned very well when we were in Atlanta together, but if he saw me in the clubhouse or on the field before a game, he'd usually stop by and ask about the farm system. He was always an upbeat, positive, highly energetic type of person who was very focused and didn't engage in a lot of small talk. He and Bobby are similar.

The news from Kansas City broke on May 31, 2006, that Allard Baird had been fired and that I was the new general manager. I would assume the role of the organization's sixth GM on June 8, right after the draft.

"We went down fighting," John, ever the encourager, told the Associated Press after the announcement. "I was trying to convince him to hang on for a few more years till I hang up my spurs and be considered for this job. We made a strong offer to keep him. But he feels he's ready to move on and take on this important challenge."

o o o

Remember the Head & Shoulders commercials from the 1980s that had the tagline: "You never get a second chance to make a first impression"? When the Royals introduced me at a press conference on June 8, 2006, I didn't get much of an opportunity to leave a first impression with the media. And vice versa.

The press conference was scheduled for 1:00 PM at Kauffman Stadium. Shortly before it started, I did an interview with ESPN. The interview itself went fine, but after we finished, the cameraman said off the cuff, "Well, congratulations, you're the general manager of a minor league team that has to play in the major leagues. How do you feel?"

The reporter shot the cameraman a look and told him, "That was uncalled for." He apologized and didn't say anything else. She'd made her point.

If only that were the worst of it.

The press conference turned into a debacle. It was the first time that Dan and Mr. Glass had been available to the media since it was announced eight days earlier that Allard had been fired and I was the new general manager, and it was obvious that the media wanted answers. The body language of many of the reporters was terrible.

Many in the room were more focused on Allard Baird being fired and less on a new general manager trying to turn things around. It seemed like every other question was negative. Most of the questions were directed at Dan and Mr. Glass.

Two radio reporters, in particular, really went after Mr. Glass and their perception of the way he handled changing general managers. It was relentless. As a result, a day or two later the Royals revoked the credentials for those two reporters. Of course that only threw gas on an already big fire.

After the press conference, Karen Kornacki, a longtime sports anchor for the ABC affiliate in Kansas City, came up to me and apologized for the treatment I received. She didn't need to do that, but it was appreciated. That says a lot about the type of person Karen is.

Unfortunately, that press conference set the tone for the next few years. As I reflected on it, I know that was partly from the frustration felt by both media and fans. But it made me wonder what type of hornet's nest we'd stepped on. Allard Baird and his people did a fine job. I don't know what type of general manager Allard was, but I think he's one of the best evaluators in the game, which is why he's been in player personnel with the Red Sox for several years. It doesn't matter to me why the organization was in the state it was in when we got here because we were going to write our own story. We were moving forward.

Of course, after that press conference I began to wonder what the genre of that story would be. It started to look less like a fairy tale and more like a Stephen King novel. In the upcoming weeks I continued to experience the negativity surrounding the organization, and I realized the task was more daunting than I originally thought.

There were some very good people on the baseball side, including coaches Mike Jirschele, Brian Poldberg, and Buddy Bell, and many others, plus players such as Zack Greinke, Billy Butler, and the previous year's No. 1 selection, Alex Gordon. But to turn things around we'd need a lot more.

About three weeks after I got here, John Schuerholz called me. It was a great relief to hear his voice. It felt like a parent whose child has gone away to college, and he calls out of the blue. I was convinced I'd made the wrong decision, and I didn't know how we were going to get out of it. We didn't have any big chips at the major league level. If I would've done the necessary research and analyzed

Words can't describe how special it was to share the 2014 postseason experience with my family: (from left) Marianne, Ashley, Avery, and Robert. *Photo courtesy of Dayton Moore*

the prospects, processes, and how long it would take to build internationally, as well as realized that part of the job would be restoring the community's faith in the Royals, there's no way I would've taken the job. There was no way to prepare as thoroughly as necessary from a distance. If I had a crystal ball that showed me the criticism and the hours it would take, and the separation from the family, I'm quite certain I wouldn't have left Atlanta. Good leadership and sitting in that GM's chair for the first time requires an extreme amount of commitment, energy, and passion.

As I expressed frustration and anxiety to John during that call, and kept stressing the importance of building our farm system in Kansas City, he said, "Dayton, there's no doubt in my mind you guys will build a great farm system. However, you can't lose sight of the importance of being competitive and having a winning major league team."

And nobody has built a winning major league team more than John. His directive kept ringing in my mind six years later as we were processing the Wil Myers trade. Ultimately, we had to win at the major league level.

o o o

Doubt had crept in during the summer of 2006, but the flip side is that we had a love and passion for the team, and we wanted everyone who's ever been associated with the Royals, and most importantly our fans, to experience the same passion and, eventually, the joy of a championship. All of our success is tied together, from people who are employed by the Royals, people who cover the Royals, and people who are fans of the Royals. I shared with the media at the time that I wanted them to cover a winner.

Writers and reporters want to cover their beat on the biggest stage. So, I said, "Let's support one another. There'll be a few things I can't talk about—very few—so give us the benefit of the doubt. Otherwise I'll be completely transparent." In some circles that worked. In others it didn't.

Things were going to get much tougher before they got easier. As we did occasionally in Atlanta, Marianne and I would take long walks together after games. Those negative voices that said we couldn't win here were beginning to creep in. But even in those private moments of self-doubt, I started to tell her, "We didn't come here to lose. We're going to win."

We were all-in. There was no looking back.

CHAPTER 5
CHANGING THE CULTURE

LOSING IS MISERABLE. Years of losing can wear a person down, and it has a negative effect on the entire organization, the media, and the fan base. When we arrived in Kansas City in June 2006, many in the organization had a defeated and cynical attitude. It was the sarcastic, "great, here we go again" mentality that comes with a lack of success on the field. Heading into 2006, this once-proud and model franchise had seven winning seasons since 1985, but only one (2003) since the strike-shortened season of 1994. The Royals, who battled annually for a playoff spot from 1976 to 1985, hadn't reached the postseason in 20 years. We understood completely why there was negativity, lack of hope, and frustration within our organization, the media, and the fan base.

Shortly after the 2006 season, we had a leadership retreat to help define the direction of the organization. We discussed the type of player we expected to sign and develop; our hiring processes; and how to improve morale, knowing full well the best and easiest way to keep morale high was to win. After several days of brainstorming, which included many great ideas and in-depth discussions, we decided we wanted an organization to reflect our values — an organization that we'd want our own sons and families to be a part of. That means, when hiring future area scouting supervisors, would we want that individual scout around our dinner table to discuss opportunities with the Kansas City Royals? Do we want that manager, coach, instructor, or other support staff person at every level around our sons every day? Would we want them influencing our sons? And, if our son was on this team, would we want a particular player competing with him? That only works if you hire the people who reflect your philosophies, principles, and views for building success.

From top to bottom, from Kansas City to rookie ball, we had two goals: we wanted to create a great place to work, and we wanted to motivate ownership to follow our plan for success. Our baseball operations department exists to serve our people in the field, and the only way Royals owner David Glass and his son, team president Dan Glass, were going to be motivated to follow our plan is through complete trust and understanding of our daily processes. The only way we're going to gain that trust is to communicate with them daily and be completely transparent.

The reason we were successful at developing talent in Atlanta was because it was a great place to work, with leaders who put the players and the organization first and who placed their own needs, wants, desires, and professional ambitions second. It was always about what's best for the player. Philippians 2:3–4 has always been one of my favorite scriptures on leadership. In *The Message*'s translation it reads: "Don't push your way to the front; don't sweet-talk your way to the top. Put yourself aside, and help others get ahead. Don't be obsessed with getting your own advantage. Forget yourselves long enough to lend a helping hand."

You change the culture when you have a selfless mind-set. Every decision we make needs to be about what's best for the Kansas City Royals. How were we going to create that selfless attitude and spirit here in Kansas City?

LEADERS SHAPE THE CULTURE

Leaders shape the culture of their environment. That applies to all facets of life. It doesn't matter if you're talking about a major league baseball team, a college athletic department, a Fortune 500 company, a church, or a family, the actions and attitudes of the leader shape all aspects of the organization and, most importantly, the people.

The biggest fear in any business—and especially sports teams—is when a new leader comes in, what personnel changes will he or she make? Based on the state of the Royals, some might've assumed we'd come in and clean house, and many people told me I should. Change definitely was on the horizon, but we wanted to see how people functioned in their current roles. I did not want to create an unsettled environment. I knew we'd make changes, but it might be a year or two to get all of the right people in place.

We didn't fire anyone right away, and, in fact, two of the most influential people with previous GM Allard Baird— Louie Medina and Pat Jones—are still here and continue to make strong, impactful recommendations for the betterment of the Kansas City Royals. There were other good people here upon whom we wanted to build, and they remain with the organization today, including Art Stewart, Jin Wong, Kyle Vena, Orlando Estevez, Linda Smith, Mike Pazik, Junior Vizcaino, and several coaches and managers.

Even though we didn't make immediate changes with most of the people already here, to get where we wanted to be we had to add key personnel to baseball operations. We needed new scouts throughout the United States and Latin America, and a larger player development staff, including another team at the short-season level. It wasn't a matter, though, of simply adding warm bodies. We needed to add the right people — people who understood and fit our philosophy.

Four outside people were key to our transition in Kansas City: Dean Taylor, who was with Cincinnati at the time; Rene Francisco and J.J. Picollo, both of whom were with the Braves; and Gene Watson, who had been with us in Atlanta but at the time was a professional scout for the Florida Marlins.

I actually talked to Dean and Rene before I took the job. Dean was the assistant general manager with the Reds. He was my first hire, joining the Royals about a week after me. His willingness to join me in Kansas City was crucial to my decision to come here. My background was not on the administrative side, with tasks such as contract negotiations and roster management at the major league level. Dean's vast background and willingness to come to Kansas City put me over the top in making this decision. If he wouldn't have joined me, I'm not sure it would've been a wise choice for me to come. Dean's skill set, which he gained during more than 30 years in Atlanta, Milwaukee, Los Angeles, and with Major League Baseball's Commissioner's Office, was vastly different from mine. He actually started his major league career with the Royals in 1981 as an administrative assistant in the minor league department. It was a natural fit for him to come back to Kansas City in 2006. In my opinion, Dean is one of the most talented baseball executives in the history of the game. He was the stabilizing influence in our baseball operations department from 2006 through the 2014 season. Unfortunately for us, Dean met with me in January 2014, saying he'd been thinking about retiring and he wanted to reduce his role after the season.

"You've been a huge part of what we accomplished here," I told him. "We would love to have you here in whatever capacity you choose."

He said he had some ideas that he'd share with me once he went through them. Really, I was hoping some extra time might get him to change his mind and stay with us full-time. Knowing Dean, I knew that was a slim possibility. We talked again in spring training about his role and the best way to restructure baseball operations when he left.

We announced on January 5, 2015, that Dean was retiring and would become a consultant for our baseball operations department. We'll miss having Dean around on a regular basis, along with the knowledge, expertise, and wisdom he brought to our department.

o o o

Rene Francisco joined us in August 2006 to take over our international development. From my meetings with Mr. Glass and Dan, they expected us to build and develop a strong international program, mainly in Latin America. It was a tremendous challenge because the Royals were dead last in international expenditures from 1996 to 2006, which includes staff, facilities, and resources for signing players. We were definitely way behind the industry standard. Rene came in with a plan, plus his relationships with people in the field throughout Latin American baseball are incredible. He had success in signing international players for both Atlanta and the Los Angeles Dodgers. Hiring him gave us instant credibility in Latin America.

One of Rene's first recommendations was to promote one of our current professional scouts, Orlando Estevez, to Latin American supervisor and to hire Victor Baez from the Dodgers to oversee our Dominican Academy. Orlando's passion, aggressiveness, and instincts made him a natural for this role. Victor's patience, people skills, and vast knowledge of Latin American player development made him perhaps the most critical influence on our young players.

There's been a Dominican Royals team since 1986, but in 2012 we completed a sports complex in Guerra, which can house 72 players for the summer. The dorms include everything you'd expect from a college dormitory: kitchen, computer lab, rec rooms, dining facilities, and a classroom. We also have two fields, batting cages, a weight room, bullpens, and a clubhouse as part of the facility.

We understood from day one, to be a championship organization, we must have a strong international program. With Rene's expertise and the people he has brought on board, we are in a much better position to compete for top prospects internationally.

o o o

On the same day we announced the hiring of Rene, August 13, 2006, we announced J.J. Picollo was joining us too. After serving as the director of minor leagues with the Braves, J.J. was hired as our director of player development. He understood our philosophy, what we were trying to accomplish, and how we were going to accomplish it. I knew he was capable of doing the job because he has terrific people and leadership skills. He's a great listener; he draws others' opinions out and then builds a consensus to make a decision. I knew he'd create a positive environment in player development. After a season of playing in the Yankees organization, J.J. began his professional baseball career as an area scouting supervisor with Atlanta, so he understood the area scout's vision for the player. I was confident he could share that vision with our player development staff and oversee the execution of it.

I first met J.J. when I was a coach at George Mason, and he transferred in from North Carolina State. What stands out most, even from then, is that he had a warm and inviting personality.

J.J. is now our vice president and assistant general manager of player personnel.

I'm thankful to John Schuerholz, who was gracious and supportive in allowing us to bring in Rene and J.J. right off the bat in 2006.

o o o

One other critical hire for us was Gene Watson, who joined us as a major league scout on August 16, 2006. I worked with Gene in Atlanta, where he was a professional scout. (Gene has been on the selection committee for the 2008 U.S. Olympic baseball team, and the 2009 World Baseball Classic and World Cup teams for the United States.) He is a tireless worker who's passionate about baseball, with numerous contacts throughout the game.

These men were very important for us to be able to change the culture. To sum it up, they are dedicated, passionate, and very enthusiastic about what they do. In short, they care about doing things the right way.

It wasn't easy, not that we expected it to be a cakewalk. When hiring those four gentlemen and our other leaders, we laid out a few main character traits, or questions that needed to be answered, with each candidate we interviewed, regardless of the position:

1. Are they able to apply moral principles in their lives? Meaning, do they have the proper balance and perspective as baseball men? For example, your main team's at home. Keeping this in proper balance allows you to be more successful professionally.
2. Do they understand the challenge? I didn't want to sugarcoat anything. We stressed that the job was going to be a tremendous challenge. Combining the state of where we were in the farm system, the team we had on the field, and with the economics of the game today, it was going to be one of the tougher challenges in sports today. It was going to take incredible sacrifice, personally and professionally. I would often say, "If you don't think we can win in Kansas City, don't come here."
3. They had to have a passion to win; they had to be all-in. We needed people who wanted to win as badly as Mr. Glass, Dan, and me.

The job we had in front of us was going to be a mountain of a challenge, especially in the first two or three years. So, if a potential leader lacked in those areas, he or she wouldn't have been a good fit for the Royals.

o o o

One way I can help to ensure that the other leaders shape the culture positively is to make sure we have the right people in the right place, and then let them do their jobs. One reason I was prepared for this opportunity, even though I hadn't been a general manager before, was because John Schuerholz gave all of us a lot of responsibility in Atlanta, equipped us to do our jobs, and then supported us in every way necessary.

When you delve into the early success of the Kansas City Royals, you discover a similar philosophy. Talk with someone like Hall of Fame broadcaster Denny Matthews, who's been with the club since day one. He can tell you about how owner Ewing Kauffman built a successful pharmaceutical company because he hired the right people and put them in the right place to be successful. Then, in the late 1960s, even though he wasn't a big baseball fan and had limited knowledge of the sport, Mr. Kauffman hired the best baseball people he could find and then expected them to do their jobs. One of those gentlemen was our first general manager, Cedric Tallis, who hired the best people for scouting and player development, including Lou Gorman, who had been with the Baltimore Orioles. Lou brought with him a young Orioles employee named John Schuerholz. When John was in Atlanta, he continued to use that philosophy of getting the right people in the right place. I guess you can say it came full circle in 2006.

I was a benefactor of that leadership style when I became general manager of the Royals in 1981. Mr. K had great confidence in me.

I've always appreciated and respected that, and tried to do that with other people who work with me, proven their worth, their sincerity, capability, integrity, and reliability. I haven't been disappointed very often. I believe delegation of authority is the most successful managerial method there is. Provided that you've selected the right people and made it clear what you need them to do, you expect a level of commitment that's unparalleled, plus a work ethic and honesty in their handling of responsibilities. If you're confident in your ability to do the job and ability to see the big picture, and you have surrounded yourself with good people who are ready to go to the next level and help you in various leadership positions, delegating is the best way to ensure success. That way you're taking your people and letting their energy, passion, and buy-in take your organization to higher ground.
—*John Schuerholz*

We were very focused from the beginning in 2006 on creating a great environment by making sure we had the most impactful leaders in place who understood what we wanted to do. In turn, you hope those under your guidance will thrive in those positions and become great leaders. I love the quote that's been attributed to Mahatma Gandhi: "There go my people; I must rush to catch up with them, for I am their leader." That can be interpreted different ways, but I see it as a leader who has good people around him or her, and those people take the reins and go.

ENERGY GIVERS VS. ENERGY SUCKERS

Former manager Trey Hillman and I would often talk about energy givers versus energy suckers. The idea, though, goes back to how we were trying to change the culture in 2006. We needed energy givers, people who were enthusiastic, extremely positive, and always expected good things to happen. The term "energy suckers" is self-explanatory, especially when you've been around these people: negative, bad attitude, and they often identify problems without offering any solutions. It doesn't take a lot of creativity, talent, or observational skills to simply identify a problem.

With only one winning season in more than a decade, sandwiched between two 100-loss seasons, it can be difficult to be optimistic. There were some energy suckers.

But we expected our scouts to focus on what players could do instead of what they couldn't do. We expected our managers, coaches, and instructors to teach with a very positive and uplifting style. That attitude and a positive environment would get the players through the tough times and give them a stronger desire to come to the ballpark each day. Ultimately, as you'll read throughout this book, in baseball you have to manage failure. Energy givers, men in our organization such as Rusty Kuntz, Andre David, Mike Toomey, and Larry Carter, know how to help people manage failure. We made a conscious decision to focus every day on keeping everyone positive.

Rusty Kuntz, whom I first met in 2002 when he was a roving instructor with Atlanta, is the epitome of an energy giver. I've never been around anyone as positive as him. His energy rubs off on everyone. When it was first announced that I was the new general manager in Kansas City, Rusty, who was with Pittsburgh then, called to congratulate me. He joined us after the 2007 season. Rusty is all baseball, with incredible experience and a terrific mind for the game. He has a passion and great ability to teach. As you'll read later in the book, Rusty was a major reason Alex Gordon became a Gold Glove outfielder.

Andre David, who's been with the Royals since 1998, was the hitting coach at the major league level — twice. Through all of the changes and going to the minors after being in the majors, he's remained extremely positive. He never appears to have a bad day.

Another of my early hires and someone who's a great ambassador to baseball is longtime scout and manager Mike Toomey. He was the head coach at George Washington University before starting his major league career with Pittsburgh in 1980. Mike is extremely sharp, has a keen eye for baseball talent, and brought a positive attitude and energy to our organization.

Larry Carter, who's been with the organization since 1998 and is currently our minor league pitching coordinator, is an extremely passionate and enthusiastic pitching instructor.

GRAY-HAIRED MEN

There's something to be said for experience. It's hard for many of us, regardless of our age, to put our egos away and learn from people who have wisdom from experience and aren't afraid to tell us their viewpoint. Simply trust in the experiences of others who have been there before you.

I didn't (and don't) want to hire "yes" men — men or women who are going to agree with everything I say. I want opinions from people who have conviction in their beliefs and aren't afraid to argue for a player or a situation. We want people who won't shy away from confrontation! Good organizations have the ability to debate and argue — this is what keeps relationships healthy. Conflict, when it's not personal and the end goal is for the right decision, is a good thing, and will lead to productivity. Good

As a leader, it's important to surround yourself with "energy givers," like Rusty Kuntz (center), and "gray-haired men," such as Hall of Fame scout Art Stewart (right). Rusty and Art have been critical to the building process in Kansas City.

organizations and healthy families are built and thrive on the ability to debate.

In 2013 some of our baseball operations people were having conversations at the winter meetings about trade possibilities. These discussions were getting intense. Hall of Fame scout Donnie Williams, who's one of our senior advisors, was there. Donnie, who signed with the Brooklyn Dodgers at the age of 17 in 1956, is from Arkansas and is as country as country can be. He helped break me in with the Braves, so I've known him for a long time. We decided to take a quick break from the meeting so guys could grab a drink and stretch out a bit. Donnie took me off to the side, looked me in the eye, and wagged his finger as he told me, "Look, you might not like what I'm going to say, but you need to hear it. We've got a good team here, and I'm not going to let you [mess] this thing up." You need those wise counsel guys around you. You don't want to surround yourself with "yes" men.

> *If you're honest with Dayton and work hard, you have a good chance of being here a long time. I've worked for some great general managers, but Dayton is a good Christian man, a great family man, and he treats his people well. He evaluates people's opinions, and all their input is important. He's a good evaluator of the people who work for him, but he has a lot of respect for the game and the people he's worked for. You can't ask for more than that.*
>
> *—Donnie Williams*

o o o

Art Stewart, who's now one of our senior advisors, is a Hall of Fame scout who started with the Royals shortly after the franchise started. Working with him was one of the things I looked forward to the most about coming to Kansas City. I first met Art when I was 17 years old and playing in an American Legion tournament in South Dakota. Our paths rarely crossed after that, but scouts know who the great ones are: Art is one of the best. Now that I've worked with him since 2006, I have a greater admiration for him. It's an incredible blessing to work with Art and share his experiences in the trenches and hear his wonderful stories about signing some Royals greats such as Bo Jackson, Kevin Appier, Mike Sweeney, and Carlos Beltran. In fact, one of my proudest days with the Royals was when I was able to introduce Art at his induction into the Royals Hall of Fame in 2008. There isn't anyone who's as passionate about the Royals and baseball as Art. Being able to share the 2014 pennant-winning season with him was special because of how much it meant to him. For me, sharing it with Art is right next to being able to share it with Marianne and our kids. There'll never be another one like Art Stewart.

o o o

Another mentor and a great pitching instructor was Bill Fischer, who was the Royals' minor league pitching instructor from 1975 to 1978 and in '84, and then joined us as pitching coordinator in 2007. Fish, who is a Korean War veteran, pitched for the Kansas City A's and, in 1962, threw 84 1/3 innings without giving up a walk. (That's still the major league record.) He started as an area scout with the Royals in 1968 — a year before they began playing — and eventually became a major league pitching coach with Cincinnati, Boston, and Tampa Bay. Pitchers such as Hall of Famer Tom Seaver and Roger Clemens give Fish a lot of credit for their success. I first met Fish when we both were with the Braves, and it was apparent immediately that he was a strong leader. There are many people in baseball with ideas and suggestions on how things ought to be done. Fish has firm convictions and core beliefs on how to approach pitching and the game of baseball, and he's not bashful about making his point.

When I was considering taking the Kansas City job, I talked with Fish about it. I had been bombarded with negative comments, but Fish was one of the few people who thought I could turn things around here.

I remember when he asked if he should take the job. I had a feeling Kansas City was going to make a change, but I had no idea he'd be one of the first ones to be offered. I told him, "I think you can build a farm system and be successful. It'll get better there as long as someone like you takes the job." He's a leader in his quiet way, leading by example. He's so down-to-earth, honest, and sincere that it makes you wonder if it's a front. It's not. He's such a humble, ordinary guy. Dayton brought the philosophy from Atlanta with him and fit it to his style. He could be an executive with any type of company. He gets the most out of people around him. Everybody wants to come to work for him.

—*Bill Fischer*

I've known Bill Fischer, who started his coaching career with the Royals in 1968, since when we were with Atlanta in the 1990s. Fish is a strong leader with firm convictions on how to approach pitching and the game of baseball. *Photo courtesy of Dayton Moore*

SYNERGY

In terms of our building the Royals, synergy is making sure that there's a strong cohesion between scouting and player development, and having men who are willing to do whatever the organization needs them to do to make that bond stronger.

One of the cancers for a baseball organization is the fighting between scouting and player development. A player gets signed because a scout believes in him, but the minor league coach doesn't have the same vision for the player. The scout loses trust in player development because he feels they haven't helped the player, and the player development person loses trust in the scout because he doesn't believe the player has an upside for being a major leaguer. We have several men in our organization who bring this type of synergy.

Mike Arbuckle, who joined us after the 2008 season, is a lifer in scouting and player development. He oversaw those departments with the Philadelphia Phillies as they were building their championship years with homegrown players, including Chase Utley, Jimmy Rollins, Cole Hamels, and Ryan Howard. So he came here with a strong background in both scouting and player development. I've known Mike since he was a scouting director for the Phillies and I was an area scout with the Braves. He's a very focused and talented baseball man.

We hired Lonnie Goldberg to be our director of baseball operations in 2008. Lonnie was the national scouting supervisor for the Braves. He has a reputation and a proven track record of being a gifted evaluator. He was instrumental in creating a cohesive atmosphere here between scouting and player development, primarily because of his relentlessness to pursue talent and to see players reach their potential.

Scott Sharp, who is the assistant general manager of baseball operations, is very patient and steady, extremely detailed, and intelligent. In player development you need patience, understanding, and calmness. Scott Sharp provides terrific leadership in our front office.

With these men I knew they'd help bring cohesion from the front-office side. Ultimately, though, the area scouting supervisor and the minor league manager are the ones who have to make those relationships work. The directors are the catalysts behind it, but the area scouting supervisor and the minor league manager are most important for creating that synergy between departments. Two men who have exemplified that on the player-development side are Brian Poldberg and Mike Jirschele.

When we arrived in 2006, Brian Poldberg, who'd been with the organization at various levels since 1987, was the first-base coach on manager Buddy Bell's staff in Kansas City. The next year, Poldberg was Buddy's third-base coach. After that season we reassigned Poldberg, who'd been on the major league staff since 2004, to Double A Northwest Arkansas as the Naturals' manager. We then stepped out on a limb and, after reassigning him to the minors, asked him to humble himself a little more by coordinating the major league camp. Most guys would be bitter about being reassigned to the minors, let alone then being asked to run the major league camp. Do you want to know Poly's reaction when he was asked? "No problem, I'll do whatever you need me to do."

Besides his gracious handling of the situation, you know what he did when he was reassigned? He worked to build a winning culture at our Double A level and went on a four-year postseason streak, including the 2010 league championship. In 2014, after we promoted Mike Jirschele from manager of Triple A Omaha to major league third-base coach, Poly took over the Storm Chasers and led the team to its second-straight Triple A National Championship.

Jirschele's tenure with the Royals is similar. He joined the organization in 1992 as the manager of the Royals' rookie team. During the next 20-plus years before he joined the major league staff in 2014, Jirschele also managed our High A team, served as a roving infield instructor, and managed Triple A Omaha twice. Managing in Triple A, especially in the Pacific Coast League, is not an easy task. For one thing, you have players at various stages of their careers. Some are ascending to the majors, while others are on just trying to hold on but are frustrated because they think they should be in the majors. Travel is normally rough in the minor leagues, but I think it's hardest in the PCL because teams extend from Tennessee to California, and Washington to Louisiana. Through all of that, Jirsch led Omaha to four division titles and two league championships.

Jirschele had a strong reputation of being a Royals-oriented person. After working with him for a few years, indeed I saw that he demonstrated a selflessness to put the organization first with everything he did. So I was excited when we were able to make him a part of our major league staff in 2014. He is a terrific third-base coach.

Jirsch is highly respected by the players, and if there's one thing I've learned, it's that you can't fool the players. They develop a strong sense of respect and admiration for their managers and coaches when that person has demonstrated that he cares. That respect for Jirschele is a testament to his character and his ability to put others first, which probably comes from his family life growing up. Mike was the third of eight children — four boys and four girls — to Don and Mary Jirschele in Wisconsin. The three other sons were diagnosed with muscular dystrophy. That's been a major part of Mike's life from the time he was a young child. The three brothers lived into their forties, but all three, plus Mike's mom, died within a nine-year period. Our players don't necessarily know that story, but they do know how much Jirsch cares about each one of them and this organization.

When we've asked them to change positions within the organization, Poly and Jirsch, both of whom are multiple winners of the Dick Howser Award that goes to the organization's player development person of the year, have a common answer: "Whatever you want me to do to help the organization."

Without question, through their selflessness, Brian Poldberg and Mike Jirschele have been as impactful and responsible for our success as anybody else in the organization.

o o o

Along the lines of scouting and player development, one of the areas we wanted to improve and develop was the analytical department. I grew up in a traditional way in baseball. Because the "Moneyball" era was becoming big in the game, analytics, or sabermetrics, became an important part of scouting and player development. Statistics have always been important for both a player's personal valuation and validating the judgment of a scout.

Knowing that Mr. Glass expected us to build a model organization in every facet, we began to dive into the analytical world. Immediately in 2007 we began to hire outside consultants to advise us in the area of analytics. Enter Mike Groopman as an intern in 2008, whom we then kept on board full-time in 2009. Mike, who held internships with Cincinnati, the New York Mets, and MLB's labor relations department, developed our analytical department. Now, whenever we're trying to make a decision about a free agent, a possible trade, or before the draft, there is an in-depth statistical analysis that takes place. As John Schuerholz used to tell us, "Stats don't lie." It's an area where I have grown professionally. In order to be successful, we must explore every talent pool and utilize all sources of information.

THE ENVIRONMENT

As a part of changing the culture and bringing championship baseball to the fans of Kansas City, the overall environment throughout the whole organization needed to improve. If we expect players to join the Royals out of high school, they must believe and trust that they are joining an organization that has high standards.

Most people who read this book won't know the name Jeff Davenport. Jeff started with the Royals in 2000 as hitting coach for our short-season team in Spokane. After that season he became the assistant to our traveling secretary, eventually moving up to senior director of team travel in 2005.

"Davy" is the perfect example of someone thriving in his environment. During my time of getting to know our people in 2006, I found out that Davy and I had a mutual connection, Jeff Blauser. Davy was the bullpen catcher for the Chicago Cubs in 1999, and one of the Cubs players that season was Blauser, a former Atlanta player. I found out that Davy had been a minor league player and hitting instructor in the Arizona Diamondbacks' minor league system, and I thought he might want to go into baseball operations.

So, after the 2006 season, I invited Davy and J.J. Picollo to the house to discuss the possibility of Davy taking a front-office job in our player development department. From his initial reaction, I didn't get the impression that he was overly thrilled with the possibility. Basically, he enjoyed what he was doing, although he was willing to take on additional responsibilities.

> *Turning him down was one of the scariest things I've ever done. He had already made a couple moves by then, so in the back of my mind I figured that by talking to me about another job, he must be bringing in someone to be the traveling secretary. I had to do a lot of soul-searching for about 10 days because I was convinced he wanted me out of the job. Eventually, I realized that everything I'd been hearing about Dayton was that he's an up-front, honest person, so I was going to be honest. I went into his office, scared to death. I said, "I just need to tell you where my heart is, which is on the operations side." He sat back in his chair, and I was convinced he was going to drop the hammer right then. He said, "I guess I got a bad read on this; I thought you'd want to be on the player development side. I don't have a problem at all with you continuing as traveling secretary. But I think there's definitely more you can do to contribute to what we're doing here." That meant a tremendous amount to hear that.*
> —*Jeff Davenport*

One area where we really needed help was in our clubhouse. It was bland and needed an identity, a personality. A problem I had with it was that there wasn't any type of emphasis placed on the championship Royals teams of the 1970s and '80s. When I asked around, I was told, "All anyone talks about is the Royals of old, so we took the opposite approach because we want our own identity." As with any family, the history is an important part of who we are as an organization. We have a rich history that I wanted instilled in our players. Why would you want to forget that? In addition, though, since we're talking about the clubhouse where they spend a lot of time, I wanted them celebrated as major league players.

Davy, being an ex-player and ex-coach, had a great feel for what we needed to do, so we added to his job title: senior director of team travel/clubhouse operations. The job is a perfect fit for him.

He helped oversee the clubhouse portion of the Kauffman Stadium renovation and made sure that yesterday and today are being celebrated. Now, instead of only one "motivational" poster hanging in the clubhouse, which is what was there when I arrived, the main clubhouse has large framed photos of each current player playing in a Royals uniform. Most of the photos in the players' lounge feature Royals legends having fun with each other. For instance, there's a picture of a champagne celebration in 1985, and guys like Bret Saberhagen and Hal McRae joking around. The players' kitchen has large framed covers from when the Royals have been on the cover of *Sports Illustrated*, and a few covers from the team's *Gameday* publication.

As the players exit the clubhouse to go to the field, they walk down a long hallway that has championship banners hanging on one wall, and more than 25 black-and-white photos from great Royals moments on the other wall. At the end of that hallway, when they're walking into the clubhouse from the field, there are large framed photos of George Brett and Frank White, the two players who have had their numbers retired. Jeff has created a great, unique environment that helps make our players proud to be with the Royals.

Jeff Davenport was instrumental in another thing we've done to help boost morale and celebrate accomplishments. Thanks to his input, we provide players with pieces of memorabilia when they reach a milestone, including their first game in the major leagues. For instance, on August 5, 2014, Alex Gordon got his 1,000th career hit. Davy put together a nice display box that includes the ball and bat, six of Alex's baseball cards, and the Royals logo. When a player makes his major league debut, Davy has the player's jersey and that game's scorecard framed.

We've extended those types of celebrations beyond the players, though. When Zack Greinke won the Cy Young Award in 2009, we created posters and other memorabilia honoring Zack, and then we made sure everyone in the organization received those pieces of memorabilia. We celebrated our Gold Glove winners by creating gold baseballs for people in our organization. If a scout signed a player who eventually reached the major leagues, we celebrated that scout with certificates and signed jerseys. To some, those might seem like small gestures, but they're huge ways to help everyone realize that we're all in this together. Everyone matters.

One story I'll never forget that goes along with changing the attitude here and making people feel special happened during our first spring training together, in 2007. [Dayton] told me that he wanted to make sure guys had plenty of gear—hats, sunglasses, shirts, et cetera— in their lockers. Dayton made a point of making sure the players had more than they could want. We were out for a run late one day on one of the fields, and he mentioned how we'd done the right thing by making sure the players had that gear. Suddenly he stopped running, took off his sunglasses, and said, "Listen, as long as I'm here, don't ever stop pushing, everyday, to make our people feel special. Obviously, we have a budget, but don't stop pushing to make them feel special. Improve their quality everyday because if we don't have a good morale, we won't have a good culture." He was practically thumping me on the chest to get his point across. I haven't forgotten it, and it's made a big difference.

—Jeff Davenport

o o o

Another person in our organization who took a suggestion and ran with it was Nick Leto, who's the manager of our Arizona operations. The first time I visited our spring training home in Surprise, Arizona, I was, well, surprised. Much like the Royals clubhouse at Kauffman used to look, display of the Royals name, logo, and past were few and far between. If you saw the stadium and drove up out of curiosity, you would have to hunt to realize that it was our spring training home. Even inside, the building was plain and nondescript. It could've just as easily been your dentist's office.

Nick, who came to the organization in 2008 after working for Detroit and Atlanta, took charge of renovating the complex with everything from plastering the Royals logo everywhere to adding reminders of our history and our future. It starts as soon as you proceed to the main building in the complex. To the right there are life-sized photos of our Royals Hall of Fame players. Once you enter the main building, you're greeted with the Royals logo and photos celebrating past seasons, key moments, and great players. Much like our clubhouse at Kauffman Stadium, the major league clubhouse at the complex in Surprise features framed photos of Royals greats and current players. The minor league players walk down a hallway that, on one wall, has a collage called "Homegrown," which features framed photos of players who have come through our system and are playing in the major leagues. On the other wall, which is titled "The Road to the Major Leagues," hang framed jerseys from each of our minor league affiliates. For a 20-year-old young man who wants to make it to Kansas City, these are ways to motivate and serve as reminders.

I think the most important "decoration" in the building is the Homegrown wall. It's a wall that's a source of great pride for scouting, player development, front-office, support staff, and the athletes. It's fun to show it off to outsiders and/or new prospects. That's important because of the large emphasis that Dayton puts on the environment for the players and staff. It's just one of the reasons I think Dayton is a world-class leader. There's no doubt in my mind that he ranks as one of the great leaders in any business in the world right now—I feel that strongly. He's an incredible listener who pushes us all very hard, but also makes us a part of everything and allows us great freedom. It's not an environment for everyone, but it's the best environment for quality people who want to learn and grow as people and in their careers. This is truly a very unique place to work. I'm very honored and fortunate to work for such an great human being.

—Nick Leto

The whole experience in Surprise is a tribute to the Royals. Outside, we named the three fields after the three men who've had their numbers retired: George Brett, Dick Howser, and Frank White. Our current players see those names every day. And then, at the minor league complex, the watch tower was renamed after Hall of Fame scout Art Stewart.

In an attempt to get the former Royals greats to spend time with the current players, we created in 2007 a "guest instructor" program during spring training. It gives current players at all levels of our system the chance to learn from Royals alumni. The next year, in 2008, we felt it was important to have an awards ceremony to celebrate the accomplishments of individual players from the previous year. Taking that a step further, we created awards in the names of past Royals greats that would highlight their standout qualities. So we have these awards, which go to the top players throughout our organization:

- George Brett Award: overall minor league player of the year
- Paul Splittorff Award: overall minor league pitcher of the year
- Frank White Award: top defensive player in the system
- Willie Wilson Award: top baserunner in the system
- Mike Sweeney Award: the player who best represents the Royals organization on and off the field
- Dick Howser Award: player development person with most profound impact on the system in a given year
- Matt Minker Award: affiliate front office or staff member who best represents the ideals of Matt Minker, including hospitality, work ethic, attentiveness to players/fans/front office, etc.

With those awards and the guest instructor program, we've taken the talents, ingredients, and expertise of former players and passed them along to younger players. We did those things early in our time here to strengthen the environment. Baseball is a family, and successful families understand the importance of celebration.

Besides celebrating our history, though, all of those changes at Kauffman Stadium and in Surprise set a personal, subliminal challenge to our current players to see the expectations set before them.

We needed that positive environment to extend to our minor league affiliates, too. What are the cities like where we have our minor league affiliates? Where do the players live when they play in these cities? How are the field conditions at our home parks? Our evaluation even included the players' food and the support staff in the clubhouse. How can we make those things better? We worked at developing strong relationships with the general managers of our minor league teams so our players could have the best environment possible.

We are fortunate in this organization to work with very talented people within those minor league organizations. It's a true partnership in every sense of the word.

o o o

The overall environment extended to Kauffman Stadium with the renovations, which had been approved before I got here. Early on I was involved with Dan Glass and Kevin Uhlich, our senior vice president of business operations. I'll never forget the day we had a meeting at

Populous, the architecture firm that was handling the renovations, and I had to keep excusing myself because my phone was ringing off the hook. So I was in and out of the meeting. I knew that the meeting and being involved with the renovation was important, but I had nothing of substance to add to the process or the discussion. Kevin and Dan clearly had the vision of what they wanted in a renovated ballpark, so I asked respectfully not to participate in the process. I left it to Dan and Kevin and Populous, and they did a spectacular job.

A great memory was 2009, when the players stepped into the clubhouse and onto the field. When they saw the completed renovations for the first time, they had the giddiness of little boys playing under the lights for the first time.

FREEDOM IN TRANSPARENCY

As part of changing the culture, I have stressed transparency in myself and our organization in order to achieve long-term success. Transparency, I believe, is very important in all areas of life because it's a great way to build trust. You're going to get exposed in life anyway, so you might as well be open about your flaws and mistakes. You have to know what you don't know.

Being transparent with the Royals meant that we were going to talk to our fans about everything we were doing. We knew that would open us up to criticism. Have you ever been *willing* to do something that you knew could open you to a lot of criticism? It's much easier said than done. I didn't handle the criticism well early. My German roots and the competitor in me wanted to fire back. But our fans had gone through more than 20 years of losing. We needed to explain to them what we were trying to do…explain the process of building. We wanted our fans engaged and invested emotionally in our ballclub. It's okay to let them second-guess what we're doing and send mail. When someone would send a letter to me that was well thought out and not just spewing a hateful message, I'd respond and explain where we were and where I thought we were going. Our fans had to trust us, and you can't build trust with another person unless you're willing to be vulnerable.

I didn't sugarcoat the situation then, so I won't now: we did not have a good culture in Kansas City in 2006. There might be several reasons for that, but ultimately it comes down to winning and losing. Winning can hide a multitude of potential problems in your organization. There's no hiding when you're losing. But in 2013, as a result of the culture changing throughout the organization, the product on the field in Kansas City was improving. The transformation of the fans' experience was complete with a great "new" Kauffman Stadium and an exciting team on the field.

LEADING YOURSELF WELL

This journey has showed me the importance of leading myself well. If I'm not leading in my personal life, it's going to be difficult to lead other people. For me, it's come down to three things:

1. Your Team's at Home. I'll never forget one time when I was in charge of international scouting for the Braves, a job that demanded a lot of hours and travel. Marianne and I were walking through our neighborhood, and she said, "You know, you guys are so addicted to baseball it's like a cult." The term *cult* has always scared me, so I asked her what she meant. She explained, "You're all-consumed with baseball, 24/7. That's all you talk about. You're traveling all of the time, and when you're here you're always on the phone." She was right; it had taken over our lives. It's easy for that to happen because it's something we've been doing all of our lives. Phil Dale, a friend and longtime scout with the Braves, would ask me how the team's doing. Of course, I'd start talking about some of our players. "No, you idiot," he'd say, "your team at home." Over the years, I've worked to make family a priority. After the 2013 season, when we won 86 games and were on the door of the playoffs, people started to say that, if we didn't get to the postseason in '14, Mr. Glass needed to clean house. Instead of feeding into that talk and adding more pressure, I made sure that our family took a two-week trip with our church to the Holy Land. The timing coincided with the general manager meetings, but to me it was more important to be with my family and experience that trip to see the Bible come to life for our kids.

2. You Have to Forgive, Every Day. If you don't forgive on a daily basis, you'll become bitter and consumed with the wrong things, creating a feeling of consistent misery. There'll always be someone saying or writing something negative, so I have to forgive. The ultimate example of forgiveness is Jesus. The disciples followed him every day, saw the miracles, and they still betrayed him. What did he do? He forgave. So lose your ego. For me, without my faith, I'm not sure I would have the ability to forgive and start with a fresh and positive attitude each day.

3. You Can't Quit. My first year in pro baseball was 1994. As much as I love this game, since it is so consuming, I've gone through periods every year since '94 wondering if this is what I want to do for the rest of my life. The game will beat you up and can become very discouraging. You have to persevere. Athletes don't feel like giving their best effort, mentally or physically, each day, but they have to push forward. The same applies for everyone else in this business.

Those three things can apply to each of us in our daily lives: get your priorities right, forgive every day, and don't quit.

CHAPTER 6
ORGANIZATIONAL HARMONY

IN 1996 THE LATE BOB BRINER wrote a book titled *The Management Methods of Jesus*. It's a short but very good book in which Briner uses about 50 modern-day leadership scenarios and ties them to some of Jesus' teachings.

That book impacted me enough that, as we were working to change the culture of the Kansas City Royals, I tweaked some of Briner's topics and developed a model of Organizational Harmony.

Organizational Harmony

Settle Disputes Quickly

Be Responsive

Give People More Than They Expect

Stand Up For Your People

Remain Calm in the Eye of the Storm

Share the Glory

Practice One-on-One Communication

Royals

Organizational harmony doesn't mean that we're standing around, holding hands, and always agreeing. On the contrary, organization harmony exists only if everyone feels as if they can freely express their opinions and offer outside-the-box ideas. If they feel like they can never weigh in, they'll never buy in. The core beliefs are basic, but the premise is that you want everyone on the same page. In baseball it's tough enough to compete against the 29 other teams in major league baseball; you don't want to compete against 30.

As a leadership team, we strive to be accountable in the following areas:

Settle Disputes Quickly. Disputes within the organization are more harmful and disruptive than with people on the outside. *"Settle matters quickly with your adversary who is taking you to court. Do it while you are still together on the way..."* Matthew 5:25

Be Responsive. With all the different ways to communicate today, there's no excuse for not responding quickly to the people with whom you work most closely. You may not have the answer right away, but it's okay to say, "I don't know, but I'll find out and get back with you."

Give People More Than They Expect. Have a positive, generous attitude. *"And they exceeded our expectations: they gave themselves first of all to the Lord, and then by the will of God also to us."* 2 Corinthians 8:5

Stand Up for Your People. This is a team! We all make mistakes and we all need to be accountable. As an example I discussed earlier, with a baseball organization, scouting has to be the biggest defender of player development, and player development has to be the biggest defender of scouting. *"If* *either of them falls down, one can help the other up. But pity anyone who falls and has no one to help them up." Ecclesiastes 4:10*

Remain Calm in the Eye of the Storm. This is the most challenging one for me because of my intense nature. I've had to apologize more than once to members of my staff for losing my cool. Former major league catcher and current Royals special assignment coach Jason Kendall has helped me learn to manage my emotions. The storms will come, professionally and personally. The question is how you'll deal with it. *"A furious squall came up, and the waves broke over the boat, so that it was nearly swamped. Jesus was in the stern, sleeping on a cushion. The disciples woke him and said to him, 'Teacher, don't you care if we drown?' He got up, rebuked the wind and said to the waves, 'Quiet! Be still!' Then the wind died down and it was completely calm." Mark 4:37–39*

Share the Glory. All of our success is tied together. We won the 2014 American League championship because of great support from ownership, the vision of our scouts, the expertise of our player development staff, the preparedness and toughness of Ned Yost and our major league coaching staff, the unparalleled commitment of our medical team and strength/conditioning coaches, led by head athletic trainer Nick Kenney and strength coach Ryan Stoneberg, and a support staff that conducts themselves in a highly professional manner. *"I have given them the glory that you gave me, that they may be one as we are one." John 17:22*

Practice One-on-One Communication. The absolute best way to get your point across is through one-on-one communication, not through text messages or emails. It's often necessary to make a presentation to the entire organization, but you need to make sure you're having one-on-one conversations with the right people in order to influence change.

o o o

To be a good leader you have to be a good servant. That type of servant leadership is something I've always preached. There is nothing that Dayton requires of his people that he wouldn't do himself. He's really fair in his assessment. He holds everyone to a high standard, and they appreciate it. People like to have high expectations placed on them. Besides the high expectations, though, he builds confidence in the people who report to him. They understand who he is, what he believes in, and what he stands for. People love to follow a guy like that because they know in the end they're going to win. I think Dayton has the qualities to be a good leader in any business.

—David Glass

The principles that create organizational harmony can apply to any department in any type of business, but for the Royals it all starts with the relationship between the general manager and the manager. For organizational harmony to exist, that relationship must be one of trust and an unwavering cooperation. This relationship must be dedicated to getting things right. The manager puts his reputation on the line every night for all to see, which the general manager must understand. Therefore, the general manager is accountable for providing the manager with players who have a strong desire to win and whom the manager can best use for his style.

It's important to us that every player throughout our organization has—or at least develops—a desire and passion to play for our major league manager. On the flip side, the manager must have a sincere appreciation for the expertise of every member in the organization. The manager's kindness and respect toward our scouts, minor league managers and coaches, medical team, support staff, and entire front office is paramount. The example he sets carries a ton of weight throughout the organization because his behavior will be modeled by others.

> *I don't know where we can find a better leader than Dayton. He's as solid as granite, through and through. He's hardcore, but he's a special person. He has great people skills, he's a wonderful family man, and an incredible baseball man.*
>
> —*Paul Snyder*

BUDDY BELL

In Atlanta, I admired the relationship between John Schuerholz and manager Bobby Cox. A few weeks after I arrived and began working with current manager Buddy Bell, I envisioned us developing that type of long-lasting relationship with the Royals.

Allard Baird hired Buddy as the club's manager in 2005. Buddy is an extremely gifted baseball man with a strong presence and a great heart for baseball. He had a mutual care and respect with his players.

Toward the end of the 2006 season he was diagnosed with cancer, and he missed the last 10 games after having surgery. Buddy is as tough as anyone I've met in this game, but as anyone who's fought cancer can attest, it changes a person's priorities, even when they get a clean bill of health. After the cancer, Buddy began to reassess his life and wasn't sure if he wanted to continue to manage. He

Buddy Bell (right) was already managing the Royals when I became the general manager in 2006. He is an extremely gifted baseball man with a great heart for the game.

came back in 2007, but in mid-July he told me he was going to step down at the end of the season.

Originally, Buddy was going to stay with the organization as a special assistant in our baseball operations department, but he got an offer he couldn't refuse from another former team, the Chicago White Sox, and he went to work for them. He's currently their vice president of player development.

Being able to work with Buddy Bell during 2006 and all of 2007 was and always will be a very special time during my baseball career. He remains a great friend today and supportive of what we're doing in Kansas City.

TREY HILLMAN

As we were looking for Buddy Bell's replacement, one name that rose to the surface was Trey Hillman, who was a proven winner everywhere he'd been. He hadn't been a major league manager, but he won championships as a manager in nearly every level of the New York Yankees farm system, including Triple A. To make it to the top of the Yankees farm system and win under that scrutiny is impressive. He then went to Texas as their farm director, and they won. He went to Japan and won the Japan Series championship with the

Things didn't work out as we anticipated with Trey Hillman as manager because our team wasn't quite ready to win. But I firmly believe he'll get another opportunity to manage in the major leagues.

Nippon Ham Fighters. Trey had an impressive résumé that made us think he was the perfect candidate.

Knowing that Trey was a strong candidate, Rene Francisco and I went to Japan to meet with him as best as we could under the radar. It was amazing because Trey Hillman was a hero in Japan. His face was on billboards — there was even a restaurant named after him. He was exceptional in our interview, possessing the characteristics and philosophies we wanted. As we did our due diligence, I couldn't find anyone in the game of baseball who could say anything negative about him. In our minds, he was absolutely the right manager for our team at the time.

Unfortunately, we hired him when we weren't ready to win yet, which is a baseball operations department failing — not a Trey Hillman failing. During the 2010 season, things weren't going nearly the way we expected them to. We got off to a slow start and one of the big pieces of our future, Alex Gordon, was being sent down to the minor leagues to learn a new position. Trey and I discussed the situation, and I consulted Royals owner David Glass and his son, team president Dan Glass. Ultimately, in May we decided we needed to make a change. Because of Trey's heart and compassion for our team and this game, it was a difficult decision, and my emotions came out during the press conference when we announced the firing.

Trey handled everything with incredible grace and positivity. He is an incredible leader, and an extremely talented and smart baseball man. He is definitely someone who fosters organizational harmony.

As of the writing of this book, Trey is the bench coach in Houston for manager A.J. Hinch, but there's no doubt in my mind that he will get another opportunity to manage.

NED YOST

When we hired Ned Yost as a special advisor to baseball operations in January 2010, a lot of people assumed that it meant Trey Hillman's days were numbered, or that we were getting Ned in house so he could step in as manager if and when we fired Trey. That simply wasn't true. Yes, Ned had been a manager in Milwaukee and a coach in Atlanta, but Ned's experience in this game and his ability to evaluate talent made him a natural fit for us in scouting and player development.

Once we knew we were going to make a managerial change, Ned emerged as a great candidate based more on his background in baseball and his character traits than on his previous four months in our baseball operations department.

Ned is possibly the most positive and optimistic person that I've been around. You can debate any manager's strategies and question some of his moves during a game, including Ned's, but remember what former Royals manager Dick Howser said. After the Royals lost Game 2 of the 1985 World Series, some people felt Dick left pitcher Charlie Leibrandt in the game too long instead of going to Dan Quisenberry. Howser said, "Second-guessing is part of the game. I do it, too. It's my job to make decisions, then explain them and then take the heat." That's Ned. And, much like Dick, Ned is a great competitor. You have to have those traits—optimism, competitiveness, and a positive outlook—in baseball.

Even though Ned is incredibly optimistic, as a leader trying to foster organizational harmony, it's imperative that I pick the correct words and even body language to use around him. Even though a game may not have turned

Ned Yost might be the most positive person I've ever been around, but he's also a great competitor. He was the perfect manager to guide our club through the 2014 postseason.

out the way we expected, or we're going through a tough stretch of games, I need to leave Ned — or any other manager — with something positive. "Hey, I know Gordo's been struggling, but he's always ready to play." "Moose had a rough night, but he's making great plays defensively." "Guth didn't have his best stuff tonight, but he got us through five innings." We've gone through some tough losing streaks, and we're all getting beat up from different angles, but we always need to find something positive to hang our hats on at the end of the night.

The biggest mistake we make as leaders is to take out our frustration on the group. If it doesn't benefit the person or the situation, shut up. Remember the lesson from mom: if you don't have anything nice to say, don't say anything at all. Don't interject your opinion just because you're frustrated or upset. That's a huge mistake we make as leaders.

If I can find positives, it keeps fueling Ned's strength. As Howser said, you can second-guess a manager every night. Likewise, during every single game you can second-guess a player or a coach's preparation, or an umpire's call. On a nightly basis here, though, we've chosen not to do that. That doesn't mean we don't evaluate things honestly. Every 40 to 50 games, we sit down with the manager, coaches, and other individuals close to the team and do an honest assessment of who we are, where we are, and what we need to do to improve. Beating each other up on a nightly basis doesn't benefit anyone.

Ned and I communicate with each other very well. Our interests away from baseball are different, but our values and moral principles are the same — faith, family, being team-oriented and positive, and always expecting good things to happen. We believe that the words you speak will set your path for success. Conversely, if you are speaking and thinking negative thoughts, you will create a negative path. As we're reminded in Proverbs 20:15 (NLT), "Wise words are more valuable than much gold and many rubies."

After our 2014 postseason run, we signed Ned to a one-year contract extension that would keep him in Kansas City through the 2016 season, when he's 62.

CHAPTER 7
THE PROCESS

FROM MY FIRST DAY as general manager of the Royals, we knew in this market that we'd have to win with young, homegrown talent. We weren't going to be able to be big spenders in the free-agent and international markets. We were going to have to build our minor league system.

As I've mentioned in this book, when we looked at the minor league system in 2006, we identified three main players who could impact our major league club: Billy Butler, Alex Gordon, and Zack Greinke. And then we had Mike Aviles. He was playing third base in Omaha, which was Alex's position at the time. That was it. *Baseball America* ranked our minor league system at No. 23 in 2006.

In a nutshell, the plan was this: Alex and Billy turn into productive major league players with the majority of our major league roster reflecting homegrown talent by 2012–2013. We then would sign free agents or trade for other players who would blend in with the homegrown talent to win a championship.

Based on where we were in 2006, I thought if everything went perfectly — as it usually does not, of course — it would take us eight to 10 years to be in a position to reach the World Series. That's a hard pill to swallow for our fan base because of what they'd been through. When we got here, it'd been two decades since the Royals won the World Series, which was the club's last trip to the postseason.

Overall the plan is solid, and it's worked in other places. It took Terry Ryan, who's one of the best baseball men in the history of the game, seven years to build Minnesota into a postseason team. Because of Terry's ability as a scouting director, they already had talented players in their system when he took over as general manager. The New York Yankees, who have spent as much money as anybody in free agency, struggled for many years until they committed to developing homegrown talent including Derek Jeter, Mariano Rivera, Jorge Posada, Bernie Williams, and Andy Pettitte.

> *Dayton has been criticized about the plan to develop the Royals, but it's a great recipe and it works if the ingredients are put in properly and the chef mixing it together has the proper mix of people and personalities, and they're collegial and they partner with each other and work well together. Dayton had come from here and spent his entire young administrative career in these offices. He saw what we did, he was a part of what we did, and he helped us form, as part of the leadership team, what we did. He lived it, breathed it, and understood it. When he went to Kansas City, he took it with him, but obviously he made appropriate adjustments to make it his own.*
>
> *—John Schuerholz*

o   o   o

One of my first priorities when we started in Kansas City in 2006 was to figure out the situation with Zack. He was an exceptional talent who could command his fastball better than most pitchers on this planet, but during spring training that year, he left the team because of social anxiety disorder. He was at Double A Wichita when I arrived in June. I hadn't met him yet when, about 10 days after I started, Karol Kyte, who was manager of our major league operations at the time, knocked on my door and told me that Zack was there to see me.

Wichita was off that day, so Zack drove up to Kansas City to see me. We began to chat, and he wanted to make sure that I knew he wasn't interested in being called up in September. I said, "Zack, we're more concerned about you as a person. I'm concerned about you being a great son and brother and hopefully a great husband and father one day." That was my introduction to Zack Greinke.

We put our 2007 team together as if he were not going to be a part of it. We were still trying to figure out if he was going to play. That's the off-season we acquired Joakim Soria, traded Ambiorix Burgos for Brian Bannister, and then signed Gil Meche. Even in January 2007, as Zack and I talked on the phone on a Saturday morning, I had no indication whether he was going to show up for spring training the next month.

As it turned out, he came to spring training in 2007, but he was very distant from most people. Frankly, it was hard to communicate with Zack, but I knew our pitching coach, Bob McClure, was someone Zack trusted. Bob, I felt, was the absolute right man at the right time in Zack's life. He has a very special way of communicating and managing people, with an ability to gain the trust of his pitchers rather quickly. I didn't want a lot of people trying to influence Zack, so we did all we could to pave the way for Mac to have a great relationship with Zack. Although we had Mac as an influential voice for Zack, Zack gets all the credit for seeking the necessary help to balance out his personal life so his natural talent could be freed up on the field.

At first, I didn't have a lot of interaction with Zack. I wanted to earn his trust and develop a relationship over time. The important thing for Zack and the organization was that he could come along on his time.

We moved slowly with Zack in 2007. Bob felt it'd be good to get Zack in the bullpen so he could come to the park expecting to pitch every day. I wasn't excited about that because we needed starters, and if God put anyone on this earth to be a starting pitcher, it's Zack Greinke. But I trusted Bob McClure, and he was right on with his plan. We transitioned him back to the rotation late in 2007, and he was ready in 2008.

Dayton deserves more credit than he'll take for Zack's progress, allowing Zack to take the time he needed and then getting him back on the field. Dayton's handling of that situation allowed Zack to get grounded, start over, and mature as a baseball player.
—Gene Watson, Royals director of professional scouting

It was so rewarding to see Zack win the Cy Young Award in 2009. I think he really wanted to win that award and prepared each day with that goal in mind. With the way our season was going, supporting him in that endeavor became our main focus for the last six weeks of the season. I know it was important to him, but from our medical team to the coaching staff, we were rooting hard for Zack. For the most part, he dominated.

One game that stands out in particular during that stretch was August 25 against Cleveland. Zack was nearly unhittable as he set a club record with 15 strikeouts. He pitched "backwards" in that game. It all centers on the command of his fastball, but he changed his pitching pattern, which kept Cleveland's hitters guessing. The one thing about Zack is that when we first saw him in 2006, he would try to get a swing and miss on every pitch. Oftentimes, that runs a pitcher's pitch count up. Over time Zack became much more efficient with his pitches. It was a lot of fun watching him evolve.

THE $55 MILLION MAN

Even though I felt it could take up to 10 years for us to get to the World Series, we did not want our fans to be embarrassed by the play of our major league team. It was a stressful balance because our owner, Mr. Glass (David), expected us to be as competitive as possible at the major league level without losing sight that building the minor league system was the most important part of our plan if we were going to achieve long-term success.

That's where Gil Meche comes in. We had identified him before 2007 as a young pitcher who was slated to become a free agent. We especially liked his upside: he was 27 years old with a fastball up to 96 mph and a knee-buckling curveball. He was entering the prime years of his career. When we looked internally, we didn't have another pitcher who could give us 30-plus starts. Luke Hochevar had just been signed that summer, and we didn't know what Zack was going to do.

We had the flexibility in our budget to go after Gil, but we needed to do so aggressively. Only a few talent pools exist, and free agency is one of them. This was during our first off-season, so we had to prove that the Royals would be aggressive and could win the negotiations for

When Gil Meche signed for five years at $55 million before the 2007 season, we took a lot of criticism, but we needed to show other major league teams that we could compete in the free-agent market.

free agents. As we discussed Gil's contract, we were pre-pared to go strong on four years at $48 million. Toronto was willing to go four years, and the Chicago Cubs were in big for four years. Gil's agent came to us at the Winter Meetings and said he'd sign for five years at $55 million. I called team president Dan Glass, who was supportive of the signing. A lot of people criticized us for the deal, but it accomplished two things: it showed the industry that we could compete to win the negotiations for free agents and it took the pressure and limelight off Zack.

Gil made our pitching staff better and gave us someone who could match up with other teams' No. 1 starters. We saw that from Gil immediately, when he went out on Opening Day in 2007 and beat Curt Schilling and the Boston Red Sox. Gil gave up one run and six hits over 7 1/3 innings. That was the longest outing for a Royals Opening Day starter since Bret Saberhagen went eight innings against Toronto in 1988. Gil left the game to a standing ovation. That remains one of my most memorable moments since 2006.

The first two-plus years of the deal were good. Gil was an All-Star in 2007, and then he won 14 games in '08. Both years, he made 34 starts. But his shoulder began to break down, and his next two years were rough. He made only nine starts in 2010.

In late December, I was running on the treadmill in our house when the phone rang. It was Greg Landry, Gil's agent. He just said, "I wanted to let you know that Gil's going to call you in a few minutes. He's going to retire. He'll explain everything when he calls."

Sure enough, a few minutes later Gil called. "Dayton, I appreciate everything. You guys signed me as a starter, and my shoulder will not allow me to be a major league starting pitcher anymore. I may be able to give you innings out of the bullpen, but that wasn't our agreement. I don't feel right not being able to fulfill my contract as a starting pitcher. I'm going to retire and I'm not taking a penny next season."

I was blown away. All he had to do was show up at spring training, and we would've had to pay him. But Gil, being the stand-up and accountable person that he is, didn't take advantage of the system. That was an unbelievable, selfless act on his part. I felt that he really honored our organization and, most importantly, himself with the way he handled that situation.

JOAKIM SORIA

In December 2006, we were picking second in the Rule 5 Draft. Essentially, if a club takes a player from another team in the Rule 5 Draft, it pays $50,000 for the player, and then the player has to stay on the major league roster for the following season. If he doesn't stay on the major league roster, the player's original club can buy him back for $25,000. Rumor had it that Tampa Bay, which was picking ahead of us, was going to take pitcher Joakim Soria from San Diego.

Louie Medina had seen Soria and said that Joakim had great command of his fastball, similar to Greinke, with an outstanding change-up. Louie called me before the draft and went to bat for Soria.

"Dayton, I'm telling you, this guy can pitch," Louie told me. "He can make our team."

"Okay," I said, "keep this between us for now. We'll continue to monitor everything and see what happens."

Our roster was already at 40. On the morning of the Rule 5, we released pitcher Runelvys Hernandez, the Rays picked Ryan Goleski from Cleveland, and we drafted Soria.

Louie was right! Soria quickly established himself as an elite closer who had four very good pitches that he'd utilize at any time. He could—and did—get hitters out multiple ways. Soria saved 17 games in 2007, and then appeared in 18 games in 2008 before giving up any runs. He ended that season with 42 saves and a 1.60 ERA. He was the first Royals pitcher since Jeff Montgomery in 1993 to save at least 40 games.

Several people in the organization and within the media felt we needed to trade him while there was value, but I chose not to because I felt our players needed an example of greatness. Besides that, his contract was very affordable and a team always needs a closer. Building the bullpen was going to be an important part of winning in this ballpark.

I've been criticized — and sometimes rightly so — for holding on to players too long. Soria might've been one of those. In 2010, Soria saved 43 games, but he wasn't the same the next year. In 2011 he was having some arm issues. We could've dealt him and got something in return, but you can't do that if you know there's something wrong with a player. I knew in my heart that he wasn't right, but I was hoping he'd pull out of it.

During spring training in 2012, Joakim had Tommy John surgery for the second time in his career. But I don't regret holding on to Soria. With young players, I'd rather have them a year too long and have them possibly succeed; whereas I'd rather move aging players a year too early. Some people don't agree with that philosophy, and it's probably bitten us a couple of times, but that's who we are.

After we didn't exercise Soria's option in 2013, he signed with Texas. We're blessed that he was a part of this organization. Joakim is a highly professional person and terrific teammate, plus a great husband and father. He's a guy that I want to be associated with for the rest of my life.

JOSE GUILLEN

Looking ahead to the 2008 season, we still needed Alex and Billy to turn into productive major league hitters, but to do so without a veteran hitting presence around them was going to be challenging. During the off-season there were four impact players on the market: Torii Hunter, Aaron Rowan, Andruw Jones, and Jose Guillen. The one we wanted the most out of the group was Hunter, and we were very close to getting him. In fact, it looked like we had a deal in place until the Angels came in at the last minute and made an incredible offer. We were close again after the 2014 season, but he wanted to go home to Minnesota, and I can't blame him for that. Torii is one of the great players and personalities today. It would've been an honor to have him in Kansas City, but it didn't work out. Rowan ended up signing with San Francisco, and Jones signed with the Dodgers.

One of the more interesting personalities was the impact bat we ended up signing during the Winter Meetings in 2007: Jose Guillen. Rene Francisco had known Guillen since Jose was 17 years old. He was a productive bat and exceptional talent who broke into the major leagues at the age of 19. We didn't want to go three years on his contract, but we felt we needed a veteran hitting presence to help support Alex and Billy. So we ended up being over-aggressive and signed him for three years at $36 million.

I covered the Royals for nine years as a scout before Dayton hired me on August 16, 2006. The perception was that they were very bare bones in the way they did things. By my evaluations when I was with the Marlins, the Royals had 29 fringe players on their 40-man roster. Major league free agents weren't coming to Kansas City. There were very few pieces in the system, and nothing of impact to trade. So, when we got here, we had to make signings to bridge everything together. Sure, we had to overpay Gil Meche and Jose Guillen, but we did it because they'd come to Kansas City. We offered more money to other free agents who wouldn't come.

—Gene Watson

Jose was an accomplished hitter, but we knew there'd be some maintenance. I even called Mike Swanson, who's in charge of our media relations department, and apologized to him for what we were about to do. Swanee is as good as anyone in baseball at what he does, and he said, "We'll do our best to manage it."

Jose had a very good year in 2008, with 20 home runs and 97 runs batted in. And, sure enough, there was some maintenance along the way. In May he had an outburst during a 12-game losing streak when he called out some of his teammates. A few weeks later, he made another disparaging comment about his teammates before saying he didn't care about the fans' opinions. That was about his only outburst outside the clubhouse. He was hard on the coaches and had a few tirades that fans didn't know about. But we dealt with things internally. Before we got Jose, in our environment, and where he was in his career, I thought we could positively change his behavior. I've learned through that experience that it's very difficult.

We got the hitter we thought we were getting in Jose. He competed in the batter's box, and he played to win.

I know he wasn't a fan favorite, but I will add that Jose had a tender heart and was generous with his money. All three years he was here, he found a family in the community that was struggling and he supported them anonymously.

TRADING WITH TAMPA...NO, NOT *THAT* TRADE

The majority of our trades and free-agent signings have been successful. In most cases the player we acquired or signed has given us exactly what we expected. One deal that didn't go as planned was when we sent pitcher J.P. Howell to Tampa Bay in exchange for outfielder Joey Gathright. This happened to be my first trade as general manager of the Royals, about two weeks after I started.

I told our baseball operations people that, to be successful in Kauffman Stadium, we needed speed players — players who could track down balls in the outfield and steal bases. The outfielders who have been most successful at Royals/Kauffman Stadium have had speed: Amos Otis, Willie Wilson, Bo Jackson, Brian McRae, Johnny Damon, and Carlos Beltran, to name a few.

Our scouts felt that Joey Gathright could provide that spark. In less than half of a season, 76 games, in 2005, Gathright stole 20 bases for the Rays. Defensively, Joey played in 70 games — all in center field — in 2005 and had a .984 fielding percentage after committing three errors in 186 chances. By bringing in Gathright, it would allow manager Buddy Bell to put David DeJesus in left field.

So I contacted Andrew Friedman, Tampa's general manager, to see if we could work out a deal. Although we discussed several names, we decided on Howell, who we saw as a swing man. He had appeared in 15 games — all starts — for the Royals in 2005, and had a 3–5 record with a 6.19 ERA.

We executed the deal on June 20. Two years later, in 2008, Tampa moved Howell to the bullpen, and he was outstanding for them. He had a 6–1 record with a 2.22 ERA that season and then 7–5 with a 2.84 ERA in 2009. He's currently with the Los Angeles Dodgers.

Meanwhile, Gathright, during three seasons with us, played in 258 games, batting .273 with 40 stolen bases (caught 18 times), 103 runs scored, and 69 runs driven in. His last season in the major leagues was 2011.

BRUCE CHEN

Although there are several players I could include in this chapter, one more that I want to mention is pitcher Bruce Chen, whom I've known since he was 16 years old. Bruce broke in with the Braves in 1998 at the age of 21, and pitched for nine clubs in 10 years. He had been out of the game for a year when he called Rene Francisco before spring training in 2009 and said he wanted to work out for us. The workout went well enough that we signed him. I thought we'd give him a year in Triple A so he could get his foot in the door, and then we'd release him and keep him on as a pitching coach. Five years later he was still pitching.

In 2014 we were in a tough spot and had to release him. That was a difficult moment. He had competed hard as a pitcher and led so well in the clubhouse. I tossed and turned at night during that decision, but we got stuck. At the end of August, Minnesota lit him up for six runs, and we felt we needed a fresh arm for the postseason push. We brought up Liam Hendriks, whom we had acquired from Toronto in July, and we needed a roster spot. Bruce didn't have any options remaining, so he was the odd man out.

Bruce pitched in the major leagues for 16 seasons and finished with an 82–80 career record. Whatever he decides to do next in life, there's no doubt he'll be successful.

"OH, NO, HERE WE GO AGAIN!"

I'm guessing some fans felt that way—*Oh, no, here we go again!*—when we announced that we were trading Zack Greinke to Milwaukee on December 19, 2010. After all, Royals fans had seen trades that involved high-profile players such as Johnny Damon, Carlos Beltran, and Jermaine Dye. This time it was different.

While we struggled during the 2010 season, I talked to Zack a couple weeks before the trade deadline to see where his heart was. He told me that he was a Royal and he was committed to the organization, even though he was becoming frustrated that we weren't winning. Zack's desire to win in Kansas City was evident when he told me that he thought we needed to trade some of our minor league players, who were starting to gain notoriety, to improve the major league team. For us to get better at the major league level, he was right.

Unfortunately, we didn't have the pieces in place to win, and I wasn't willing to part with the minor league players it would take to fill our needs, namely at least two pieces for our proverbial "strength up the middle." We needed an impact center fielder and a middle infielder.

Milwaukee general manager Doug Melvin, who's an exceptional baseball man, had put the Brewers in a position to make it to the postseason in 2011. Their window was open with players such as Prince Fielder, Rickie Weeks, Corey Hart, and Ryan Braun. He was aggressive to add starting pitching to go with Randy Wolf and Yovani Gallardo. Doug knew that we were looking to trade Zack. We made it very clear to Milwaukee as well as other teams interested in Zack that we wanted middle-of-the-diamond infield help and a center fielder. Milwaukee had that type of talent. The only problem is that Milwaukee was on Zack's no-trade list, which Doug knew.

Since Zack's contract stipulated that he didn't want to go to Milwaukee, I didn't know what Doug's comfort level with Zack would be. He was willing to risk it in exchange for one of baseball's best pitchers. We discussed a trade at the Winter Meetings in 2010, but left without a deal. When I got back to Kansas City I called Zack and started talking to him about Milwaukee and how it'd be a great place to play. I told him, "Doug Melvin is an incredible person and great GM. They have a lot of talent and they're going to win. I think you will get your opportunity to pitch for a winner." We had a great 45-minute conversation that night. He called me back a couple days later and said that he'd be willing to go to Milwaukee.

I called Doug and we got down to the details. He was willing to send pitcher Jake Odorizzi and center fielder Lorenzo Cain. Finally, I told him we'd send Yuniesky Betancourt if they'd send Alcides Escobar. It was a good baseball deal for both teams. I liked Escobar and Cain mainly for their speed and defense. The Brewers were giving up players of the future in exchange for a front-line starter and Cy Young Award winner who could help them get back to the playoffs. It's important that trades work for both organizations, and I think most general managers approach deals that way.

If that deal hadn't gotten done, we were prepared to start the 2011 season with Zack. We weren't going to just give him away, and Zack understood that.

Every time we make a deal or acquire a free agent, we perform the following analyses:

- Analytical — What do the statistics say about the future performance of the player?
- Scouting — How do the scouts think he'll perform based on his tools and raw ability?
- Economic — Does he fit within our economic structure over the lifetime of his contract?

- Medical — Do our medical people feel the player will remain healthy during his time in Kansas City?
- Character — Will this player fit within our clubhouse and our community? Is he a Royals-type player?

In this case, it worked. Our analytical people felt it was an upgrade. Our scouts were very high on the deal. Cain had some injuries in the past, but our medical team was satisfied. Manager Ned Yost was familiar with both players from his days in Milwaukee, so he was comfortable with the character and makeup of both players. Lorenzo and Alcides were making the league minimum, so they fit economically, but most importantly they fit our long-term plan, which was winning in 2013 and competing from beginning until end in '14.

That trade paved the way for everything we did going forward.

The thing I'll never forget about Dayton is that he came in here with a vision and a plan. He wanted to build a big amateur scouting and player development staff, and then build depth throughout the system that could be fruitful. Because of how he built the international scene and the minor leagues here in the States, he got great scouts and knowledgeable people to develop the players. That sums up why we are where we are today. And the depth in the system continues to grow. That's the key to being successful. With the market we're in, we have to develop our own and fortify with talent that we can trade for established players, when needed. Dayton never went off track from that. He stayed with the plan. He was confident it would work, and it did. He completed the picture on what we had to do to be a winner.

—Art Stewart

FACING CRITICISM

The *process* — during the past few years, that term has been given a negative connotation, especially in the media and with some fans. Not from everyone, because I think the ones who support us just aren't as loud as the detractors, but many haven't agreed with every move we've made as we've tried to build the Kansas City Royals into a consistent winner.

Everywhere I speak, someone ultimately asks how I deal with the criticism in a high-profile job. My answer: my faith gets me through. However, I don't believe I have any more pressure on me than any other man. As men we are striving each day for success in the workplace. We desire to provide for our families and give them a high quality of life. As husbands and fathers, we are competing daily for the love, admiration, and respect of our wives and children. There are times I think it might be easier for me because I get to do what I love to do. So at the end of the day, when dealing with criticism, I try to remember that kindness and love always win.

That doesn't mean I handled the pressure and the criticism flawlessly. It was extremely difficult for me in the early years. We made acquisitions that people didn't understand, and they let us know about it. I *really* wanted to fire back. Like a selfish idiot, I wanted to shout back, "Nobody wanted this job! You're lucky to have me!" I went down the trail where I wanted to say, "Screw you guys!" It goes back to pride creeping in. Jose Martinez, who was a coach with the Royals in the 1980s and then went to Atlanta, told me, "Dayton, everybody's important; nobody's necessary." Jose's words would eventually come back to me. It would've been easy to fight everyone, but I've done my

Billy Butler was one of the main pieces to our building process, along with Alex Gordon. Out of all the players in our farm system in 2006, we felt that they had the best potential to be productive major league players.

best to bring honor to our organization through my words and actions.

> There's never been a time we were looking to move on to another general manager. Dayton was the right guy. The fact we didn't get results as fast as we wanted didn't bother me. I loved his approach and integrity he brought. I knew we were going to get there. I never had doubts.... When Dayton came, we had a plan, which is basically his plan. Here's how you do it and do it the right way. He told us, "It'll take a long time to get this done, so the biggest problem we're going to have is patience to see it through." We speculated

how long it would take but we didn't set a timeline. We knew it'd take several years to develop the talent in the minor leagues and get those players through the system to the major leagues. We weren't specific in how long it would take, but we knew it'd take a while. If you talk to Dayton or to Dan, both would say it took a little longer than we expected. The 2013 season was the first time I really felt we'd be able to play in the postseason. We came close, staying in the race until the last week, but you could tell then that these players were growing up and maturing and getting better. We all got on board with the plan and said, "Let's do it." From the time Dayton came until our success in 2014, there were ups and downs, and there were some times when he took a lot of heat. Almost everyone I know in his position would've adopted a short-term strategy, probably trading a lot of prospects for major league ready players. Short-term strategies are a way out for a general manager. Dayton took hits from the media and fans, but he hung in there. Now everyone realizes that it was a great plan. I give Dayton credit for not wavering from the original plan and for weathering the criticism. I admire him for that.

—David Glass

People tell me we've shut up the critics by winning the American League championship. I'm not sure that's completely true because there will always be critics. But the question, when someone's being critical, is this: are they doing so with a critical eye or a critical spirit? If it's with a critical eye, evaluate their viewpoint. They may be helping you discover a blind spot. If it's with a critical spirit, I'm not sure you're going to change their opinion anyway, so you just need to do your best to clarify your position or explain your processes in making a particular decision. But never make excuses and always accept responsibility.

One of the players we signed in Atlanta, Onil Joseph, is now a coach in our minor league system in Kansas City. I'll never forget March 10, 2012, during spring training. I was taking a different route off the field, when OJ approached me. He said, "Dayton, God asked me to tell you something."

"Sure, what do you have, kid?"

"He told me to tell you, 'Do your fighting on your knees.'"

Those words have stuck with me ever since. Along with 2 Timothy 2:24, which, in the New Living Translation (NLT), reads: "A servant of the Lord must not quarrel but must be kind to everyone, be able to teach, and be patient with difficult people." Both have been a great source of encouragement.

Without completely realizing it, my faith was helping me weather the attacks. Even after I gave my life to Christ, I jacked it up a lot. There's no way I would've gotten through the first eight years of this journey without my faith. Until I learned to manage the attacks and the criticism well—publicly and within our organization—I needed to lean heavily on my faith.

During our 2014 postseason run, someone with Majestic, the company that runs our team store, approached me about designing a "Trust the Process" T-shirt. I declined. Even as we discussed possible titles for this book, my coauthor Matt Fulks suggested "Trusting the Process." Again, I said no.

"Don't you feel vindicated at all for sticking with—and reaching the World Series with—the plan that's been mocked as the *process*?" Matt asked.

Onil Joseph, seen here with my son Robert, reminded me in March 2012 that instead of lashing out at the media and others who were criticizing us, I needed to fight on my knees—I needed to live 2 Timothy 2:24. *Photo courtesy of Dayton Moore*

"Vindicated for what? We had great support from the Glass family and the majority of our fan base. We are very grateful that we were able to win for our fans. Weathering the criticism and winning the championship was a complete God thing."

Whenever we're facing criticism, whether it's about the Kansas City Royals or something you're doing in your job, just remain calm, and trust God to make things right.

CHAPTER 8
THE PRODIGAL SON RETURNS

IT SEEMS LIKE A HOLLYWOOD SCRIPT. A kid grows up as a fan of a baseball team that has fallen on hard times. The kid goes on to play baseball in college. Eventually he lands with his favorite team, but he does so with one lofty expectation: be the team's savior and lead them to the World Series. Since this is a Hollywood script, of course, he and the people around him endure some bumps and bruises. And he's seen as a failure. And then, in a dramatic finale, his team reaches Game 7 of the World Series.

Some could read that paragraph and assume it's about my journey with the Royals. Sure, it definitely could be. But in this case it's actually about Alex Gordon.

We talk about needing a roster largely made up of homegrown talent in order to compete for the postseason each year in this market. Alex *is* a homegrown player. He's not Frank White homegrown, but pretty close. Unlike Frank, who grew up a few blocks from the Royals' original home, Municipal Stadium, and then came up through the system, Alex was raised only about 200 miles north of Kauffman Stadium, in Lincoln, Nebraska. So each summer his family would drive down Interstate 29 for a few days to see the likes of Frank, George Brett, Kevin Seitzer, Jeff Montgomery, and so on. Cheering for the Royals is a part of Alex's DNA.

Alex went on to have an outstanding career at the University of Nebraska. It was good enough that he left after his junior year. That season he won every major award in college baseball: the ABCA Rawlings Player of the Year, the Golden Spikes Award, the Dick Howser Award, and the Brooks Wallace Award. He was a .355 career hitter at Nebraska, was in the top 10 in eight of the school's career offensive categories, and started every game during his sophomore and junior years.

Since I wasn't here yet, I can't tell you what pre-draft discussions the Royals had regarding Alex in 2005. It certainly would be difficult to pass on the top college player in the country if he could fill a need on your major league roster and he's sitting there when you draft second overall. The fact that he grew up a Royals fan and relatively close to Kansas City wouldn't factor in much. In actuality, that can be difficult for players to handle because there's additional pressure and more distractions when a player is playing close to home. For Alex, besides the normal distractions for a hometown player, he had greater pressure of being the team's "savior" because of his outstanding college career, being a high draft pick, and coming to a struggling organization. He was seen as the next George Brett, which is an impossible expectation for any young player.

Alex's first experience in professional baseball was in 2006 at Double A Wichita. That club featured many players who were seen as Kansas City's next major leaguers: Billy Butler, Mitch Maier, Angel Sanchez, and Zack Greinke. And the talented group of young players was learning from one of the greatest Royals players ever, Frank White. Alex performed as expected, batting .325 with 158 hits, 39 doubles, 29 home runs, 101 RBIs, and a league-leading 111 runs scored.

As mentioned throughout this book, from day one our plan was to draft, sign, and develop our own players in the minor leagues, and then, as they transitioned to the major leagues, surround them with talent in Kansas City. We were passionate about that—we weren't going to waiver. When we had our first organizational meetings in January 2007, we determined that Alex and Billy Butler would become productive major league players. And, in a perfect world, as they neared their prime in the major leagues, it would be crucial that we had a group of young players ready to transition from the minor leagues. Ultimately, that plan was why we traded Zack to Milwaukee before the 2011 season. We could see our young, talented players (such as Eric Hosmer, Mike Moustakas, Salvador Perez, Jarrod Dyson, Danny Duffy, Kelvin Herrera, and Greg Holland) beginning to turn the corner and become major league ready. We needed to add middle-of-the-diamond players, particularly shortstop and center-field.

We decided that Alex, who was *Baseball America*'s Minor League Player of the Year in 2006, was ready for the majors at the start of the 2007 season. He skipped Triple A, but he was ready. The challenge for Alex was that he was breaking into the major leagues without a strong supporting cast around him. This is never ideal. You'd prefer a young player transitioning to the major leagues with a strong group of talented veteran players on the roster. In the end, we trusted Alex's mental toughness.

But I will never forget the standing ovation he got at Kauffman Stadium before his first at-bat on Opening Day in 2007. Here's this kid who's expected to bring the Royals back to the glory days. And from the ovation, the crowd was ready to see it. Of course, that first at-bat was against

Boston's Curt Schilling with two outs and the bases loaded. He struck out. That was a big order for any hitter, let alone the pressure-filled debut for the organization's on-field "savior."

Gordo didn't bust out of the gate, but he had a couple of pretty good years early. As a rookie, he batted .247 with 134 hits, 15 home runs, and 60 runs scored. Defensively, he committed 15 errors. His numbers were comparable in 2008 with a .260 batting average, 128 hits, 16 homers, and 72 runs. In 133 games at third base, he committed 16 errors. Late in the season, Gordo went on the disabled list with a torn hip flexor.

It's tough when you have to put a player on the disabled list. Every situation is a little different, but, regardless, you always want to make a decision that's best for the team and the player. The expertise of the trainer and the team doctor is vital in determining the outcome. The input of the player is taken into consideration, but sometimes his competitiveness and high pain tolerance can cloud his judgment. That's why I've always wanted to have a good relationship with the head athletic trainer. The relationship and confidence in that person is very important. We had this with Nick Swartz, who was the Royals trainer for 33 years, and we have it now with our current head athletic trainer, Nick Kenney.

The next season, 2009, was a disaster for Alex and the team as a whole. After an April in which the club finished 12–10, we won six out of the first seven games in May and led the AL Central by three games before the wheels fell off. So many things went wrong that year, but one of the biggest was losing Alex for nearly half the season. On a cold Opening Day in Chicago, Alex's hip tightened on him during the pregame festivities. It felt worse as he was rounding the bases following a two-run home run in the second inning.

He tried to play through it, but we found out he had a labral tear in his right hip. We shut him down midway through the month to have surgery. In all, Gordo played in only 49 games for Kansas City that season.

I still believed in Alex and his talent even though he'd been on the disabled list in two of his first three seasons and didn't seem to be making big strides at the major league level. I learned as an area scout that you stick with the tools. Alex had power, the ability to hit for average, a strong arm, and was a very good base runner.

In the minor leagues, Mike Moustakas, our likely third baseman of the future whom we picked in the first round of the 2007 draft, was showing some power. He hit 22 home runs in 2008 and 16 in 2009.

During that off-season—in January 2010—we hired Ned Yost as a special advisor to baseball operations. Right after that we had an evaluation meeting in Kansas City with our coaches and baseball operations personnel. As we went around the room discussing our players, we came to Alex's name. There was a lot of frustration within our ranks about Alex's progress and performance as a major league player. One voice stood out, though.

"Look, Gordo will be fine. He's a great talent." It was Ned, who went on to defend Alex and his ability. Ned believes in players, which is a trait he picked up from one of his mentors, Hall of Fame manager Bobby Cox in Atlanta. For most of us in that room, our view of Gordo might've been tainted a little because of his struggles, so it was nice to get a fresh, outside perspective from Ned. He summed it up by saying, "If this guy can't succeed with us, we're in trouble."

If one scout, coach, or player development person believes in a player, you have to do what you can to provide that player with an opportunity and help him succeed. That's something I learned from Hall of Fame scout Paul Snyder. I decided we were going to remain committed to Alex, and we were going to win together. We were going to continue to believe in Alex and trust in his talent and his desire to compete.

During that whole decision process, a conversation I had in the press room at Kauffman Stadium with Detroit Tigers GM Dave Dombrowski during my first year with the Royals kept flashing in my head. It took Dave and the Tigers five years in a bigger market to turn things around. He told me, "We let everyone know we were going to do it the right way, and if we ran out of time, we ran out of time." Staying with Alex was doing it the right way. If it didn't work, it didn't work. Besides, Alex is family, and I felt it would be wrong to give up on him.

o o o

From short conversations Alex and I had during spring training in 2010, I knew he was ready to go and he wanted to have a big season. In our third spring training game, Gordo went head first into second base attempting to steal against Texas and broke his right thumb. He was scheduled to play five innings that day, and he did. We didn't know about the thumb until after he was done playing for the game.

For the third time in his major league career, Alex Gordon went on the DL. He was out until mid-April.

We'd gotten off to another slow start, winning four of the first 10 games that Alex missed. Things weren't improving for the team or for Alex. We weren't giving up on him, but we needed to come up with a solution. Alex was batting .194 with one home run. Mike Moustakas, meanwhile, was off to a great start at Double A Northwest Arkansas in what would become an award-winning year for him. Every player will face a time in his career when an opportunity doesn't present itself or when the opportunity is better for another player. We were beginning to face that with Gordon. Moose was on a fast track for the major leagues, so we had to start thinking about what was best for Alex's future.

I hadn't seen Alex before I started with the Royals, but the first time I saw him in a game, he wasn't comfortable at third base. The game sped up for him. His hands were good enough, but they were tardy getting to the ball. His feet were great but they were slow. Even on a pop-up, he'd catch it on the side of his body. His intensity and preparation were incredible and with purpose, but as soon as he went to third base, it didn't flow for him. It was even affecting his hitting. I thought, He's the No. 1 pick...from Nebraska...and the next George Brett? So I asked Dayton that, as athletic as Gordy is, if he could play somewhere other than third. "Maybe we can put him in a different spot and free up his mind," I said. "If he moved 150 feet farther from home plate, his hands and feet would be great." I thought that would allow more of Alex's athleticism to come out.

—Rusty Kuntz, Royals coach

We ask ourselves three questions when contemplating demoting a player to the minor leagues:

1. Is the player staying positive, continuing to work hard, and trying to make adjustments?
2. Do his teammates continue to believe in him?
3. Do the manager and coaching staff continue to believe in him?

The answer to all three of those questions with Alex was simple and emphatic: YES! He was accountable, he worked hard, and everyone around him believed in him. Normally if the answer to those questions is yes, we don't send the player down. But in Alex's case, we thought it'd be best for him to make the transition from third to the outfield in the minor leagues. We decided while we were in Tampa Bay in early May that it'd be best to send Alex to Triple A Omaha.

Manager Trey Hillman and I sat down with Alex after the series finale on May 2 and explained the situation to him. We told him that not only was he going to go to Omaha, but based on how we saw things shaking out with Moose and because we needed an outfielder, we planned on converting Alex to an outfielder.

"This is a tough decision but we believe it's the right decision," I said. "This isn't how we scripted out your career and this isn't what you scripted out for your career, but we need to start preparing you for a different role. You're a big part of this organization now and you're going to continue to be a big part going forward. I'm confident that this circumstance is going to help you grow as a player."

I remember the whole conversation perfectly. I hadn't been playing for a couple of days so I had a feeling something was going to happen. I got called into the office, and they told me they were going to send me down, and I was going to be changing positions. Going to the outfield was a complete 180 from what I expected, especially to have it happen during the season. But Dayton is always incredibly positive, and after he told me about moving to the outfield, he gave me examples of a few players who'd made the move successfully. It was all positive. In fact, his final words stuck with me. He said, "Make sure you and your family are doing okay, and if there's anything I can do, let me know." Again, one thing about Dayton is that he cares about you as a person, not only as a player.

—*Alex Gordon*

You never know how a player will handle that type of news, but as I expected with Alex, he understood the situation and seemed to trust us. He's always been about the team and winning, and that proved to be true throughout the upcoming months. I can't help but think that somewhere along the way — maybe not that night but at some point — he thought back to 2007. Mark Teahen, who had had a heck of year in 2006 with 18 home runs and a .290 batting average, was being pushed out of third base by Gordo. It was a selfless act on Mark's part to move around the diamond in 2007, which opened the way to Alex. Three years later, Alex, after living through that selfless act of Mark Teahen, was presented with a similar scenario with Mike Moustakas coming. He humbly accepted what we felt was best for both him and the team. It was a selfless act on his part.

Rusty Kuntz, who has a gift of teaching players, was a special assistant to the GM, plus outfield and base running

Alex Gordon became a much more productive offensive player after we moved him from third base to the outfield. He relaxed offensively once he became comfortable on defense.

coach then. We made arrangements for him to be in Omaha the next day to work with Alex.

I was going to continue the road trip with the Royals as they went to Chicago and Texas. As I lay in bed that night, unable to sleep, the thought of Alex going to Omaha weighed on me. *Alex has played only a handful of games in*

Omaha on a rehab assignment.... This time it's different because we're optioning him, and he might be there a while.... This has to be tough on his spirit.... He's experiencing his highest level of failure as a baseball player at a time when we're 10–15 and last in the division.... Our best player, our homegrown, Midwestern boy, who grew up loving the Royals and has been in the majors, is being sent to the minors in his home state, which is absolutely passionate about its sports legends.... It's going to be a zoo.... I need to be there as a show of support and personal accountability.

There was a flurry of criticism from both the media and the fans before the news about Alex broke. It was the worst it'd been since I got here in 2006. People weren't happy with my direction and leadership. If you polled most Royals fans at the time, I'm not sure there were many believers in any of us. So the news that we were sending Gordo to Omaha after three years of major league service was going to turn the flurry into an all-out blizzard.

As anticipated, there were a lot of TV people in Omaha awaiting Alex. After a long losing road trip for the major league club, I just stood by the third-base dugout and answered as honestly as I could. Alex, who isn't outspoken, handled the public scrutiny perfectly. It's easy to admire Alex and similar players because, even though he was going through those tough times, he never made excuses or lashed out at the media or the organization. He just played as hard as he could with the innocence of a young boy and worked at learning a new position.

A common trait I've learned from successful leaders is that they embrace difficult times and make the best of the situation without complaining or making excuses. I remember one of John Schuerholz's sayings: "Winners make commitments, losers make excuses." There's no doubt in my mind that Alex was going to accept the challenge and use the situation to grow as a person and as a player. Alex is a terrific leader because he leads himself well. That's the most important aspect of a leader. If you can't handle your own business, professionally or personally, others aren't going to follow you. Once you lead yourself well, you'll effectively lead others. In baseball, players can't fool other players, so transparency is incredibly freeing. Just know that you're flawed and you will make mistakes. Admit the mistakes and move on. Alex never complained or made excuses. That's held true to this day. He's never blamed a coach, a manager, or a teammate for anything. He's always been accountable and embraced every situation and made the best of it.

> Since Alex had been an infielder, I hadn't worked with him much. The first morning in Omaha, I strolled onto the field when we were supposed to meet. Alex was already in the outfield, stretching. The first thing he said to me was, "Where have you been? When are we starting?" I was surprised to see him already. "I've been here, waiting on you," he said. "I'm not going to get any better sitting at home." That's Alex. I've never been around a guy who worked that hard. As long as you had one more, he had one more. He's a perfectionist, but he wants that perfection to become a habit with the only agenda being to help the team win. Needless to say, I started getting to Rosenblatt at 10:00 in the morning to beat him.
>
> —Rusty Kuntz

That doesn't mean the switch to outfield was flawless. When I watched Gordo during his first outfield workout in Omaha, he appeared awkward and unsure. I knew he'd dedicate himself to learning the position once he accepted the change, but I'd be way out of line to say I felt Alex would be anything better than an average left fielder. I didn't see his ability to glide—he's more of a hard, forceful runner—and left field is possibly the toughest outfield position. Rusty, who's somewhat of an outfield guru, continued to work with Alex and eventually felt that he could play left field. For me it wasn't until midway through the 2011 season when I thought he'd be okay. Alex was so mentally tough through all of it that he was equipped to handle it better than a lot of guys. Did I think he'd be a Gold Glove outfielder? No offense to Gordo, but that was the furthest thing from my mind. Knowing Alex, turning into a Gold Glove winner might've been one of his goals.

That was a tough, challenging time in my life. Rusty was in Omaha for the first two or three weeks and spent as much time as possible with me every day during batting practice. He was the perfect person to have out there. If you want to talk about knowledge, Rusty Kuntz has all the baseball knowledge you could want. The funny thing is that you know he's never going to stop talking, so I learned a lot in those few weeks. If you surround yourself with good people, usually good things are going to happen. That's what I had in that situation. Dayton's incredibly positive, but if it's possible to be more positive than Dayton, it's Rusty.

—Alex Gordon

Eventually, Alex's athleticism came out defensively, and all of that helped free him mentally at the plate, I think. In 2011, his first full season in the outfield at the major league level, Gordo hit .300 for the first time in his big-league career (.303) and had career highs at the time in doubles (45), home runs (23), and RBIs (87). Oh, and by the way, he won his first Gold Glove.

Today he's regarded as one of the best outfielders in baseball. He's had so many great moments—diving catches, robbing hitters of home runs. And he has fun.

As the GM or even a fan of a team, you just want guys to give their best. That's Alex. If you're able to get to a game early enough to watch batting practice, do yourself a favor and focus on Alex. If you're with any kids who play, encourage them to focus on Alex. Most guys use batting practice simply to shag balls in the outfield. They might use it to loosen their legs a little or chat with their teammates. Not Alex—he's extremely focused. Watching his preparation is special. His pregame approach in the outfield is very similar to watching Hall of Fame pitchers Greg Maddux, Tom Glavine, and John Smoltz throw a side session. He puts himself in game situations during BP. By the time the game's first pitch is thrown, his mind and body are conditioned to be ready. He's made a lot of terrific first-inning defensive plays against the leadoff batter because his pregame work prepared him for the first pitch.

I thought Alex would be above average because of footwork and arm strength. Adding to that now, his jumps, routes, and reads are all great. When I started to see him dive for balls, I knew he was comfortable playing left field. It was so much fun watching him develop. We actually have a video from when he was warming up—we call "power shagging"—that we've turned into a five-minute reel for our minor league players. Every spring training in the minor leagues now, we show that to them and say, "If you're not doing it that way, you better start doing it. If you want to take his spot, you need to act like that." Even after his Gold Gloves, Alex gets to the ballpark at noon, works hard and meticulously, and by the time he leaves at midnight, every minute is accounted for. That's why, at the end of the day, we're showing highlight reels to our minor league players, and we're all clapping for this guy as he receives awards. He deserves all of them from his God-given talent and how he worked his tail off.

—Rusty Kuntz

Your lifestyle, habits, and choices off the field ultimately put you in a position to succeed or fail on the field. Without Alex's discipline off the field and dedication to his wife, Jamie, and their sons, Max and Sam, he would not be the player he is today.

o o o

I love the Bible's parable of the prodigal son, and I see a lot of Alex in a modern-day interpretation of the story. As the parable is told in Luke, a wealthy man has two sons, and one of them asks for his inheritance early. Once he's given his inheritance, the son sets off on a long journey, spends his money, and, humbled, eventually comes home to a loving and grateful father. When it comes to baseball, we sometimes hear of a "prodigal son" being a player with lofty expectations who doesn't perform well, and then makes a triumphant return. In Alex's case you can toss in the idea that he was lifelong Royals fan and a homegrown player.

Through the rookie hype in 2007, the injuries, being sent down to Omaha, and learning a new position, I never sensed that Alex felt pressure. That said, he needed those experiences, especially the setback in 2010, to persevere and become the four-time Gold Glove winner and two-time All-Star that he is, heading into the 2015 season. As he wrote in this book's foreword, if we had moved him to

It was a great honor to help turn on the Christmas lights at Kansas City's Country Club Plaza in November 2014, and for our family to share the time with Alex and his family. Besides being a great baseball player, Alex Gordon is a terrific husband and father. *Photo courtesy of Dayton Moore*

the outfield while he was in the minor leagues, who knows if he would've become a Gold Glove player. His resolve to come back and to turn into the player that everyone expected when he was the No. 2 pick in 2005 was incredible. There's not a player in our clubhouse who doesn't respect Gordo.

Years from now, when I think about Alex, I'm sure various images will flash in my mind, but one that will rise above the others was from the fifth inning of Game 4 of the 2014 ALCS against Baltimore. In a play that should make every postseason highlight reel, Gordon went back to the warning track in a full sprint on a J.J. Hardy deep fly ball. As Gordo stepped onto the track, he leaped back, caught the ball, crashed into the wall, and went to the ground. To leave no doubt, from his back on the warning track, he simply held up his glove. That play epitomizes the fearlessness and toughness of Alex Gordon and our 2014 Royals. That represents who we are, and it helps show that Alex Gordon is the heartbeat of our team.

CHAPTER 9
OPERATION: FLIP THE SWITCH

GOD HAS A GREAT SENSE OF HUMOR, I think.

We lost 97 games and finished 21½ games behind Cleveland in 2009. About the only bright spot was Zack Greinke winning the American League Cy Young Award. The future—our next wave in the building plan—didn't look so great at that moment, either. Some members of the media were talking about Mike Moustakas, our first-round pick in 2007, and Eric Hosmer, our first-round pick in '08, being busts. (Each player was two years away from making his major league debut.) We valued Salvador Perez, but according to *Baseball America*, he wasn't even listed among the top 20 prospects in the Carolina League. Kelvin Herrera was hurt in 2009, and Yordano Ventura had just signed in October 2008—he played with our Dominican summer team in '09.

There were times I felt lost in the wilderness. It was the first time I had to learn how to lose. I broke into professional baseball in 1994 when the Braves were in the middle of a winning stretch. My first full year, 1995, we won a World Series. I was in the front office in '96, another trip to the World Series. Same thing in '99. Coming to Kansas City to build something, I knew we weren't going to win right away. But losing 97 games in our third full season was tough to take.

Midway through the season, I got a call from Stan Kasten, who was Atlanta's team president when I was with the Braves. As he tried to encourage me, he talked about the early years of Atlanta's turnaround, and how they weren't drawing well. But, he said, owner Ted Turner was supportive, and that's all that mattered. He said, "As long as David Glass is supportive, that's what matters the most."

To say Mr. Glass was supportive was an understatement. If they had fired me at that point, no one would've been protesting on the Plaza. Instead of firing us, though, after the All-Star break, he and team president Dan Glass came to me out of the blue and offered me a contract extension. I was blown away! I didn't expect it and certainly didn't think I deserved it.

"You don't have to do this," I told him. "I don't feel we deserve the honor of an extension right now."

Mr. Glass looked at me and said, "Dayton, we're all in this together."

He understood that the media was going to jump all over this news, which, of course, would lead to more criticism, but he continued to trust in our processes and our leadership. He appreciated that we were representing the organization with class through all of the tough times.

Mr. Glass owns a baseball team for all the right reasons. He's an unbelievable historian of the game, and he knows our players throughout the organization as well as anyone else does. He knows the draft, he knows who's coming out in the draft, and where they're projected to go. He's an excellent baseball man. Mr. Glass cares deeply about the fans' experience and the enjoyment at the ballpark largely because the game of baseball holds a special place in his heart.

Dayton's a great kid with a great family who's brought a lot to our organization. I've told him that, as far as I'm concerned, we're all in this together. We're going to continue doing what we're doing. We're fortunate to have him in Kansas City.

—David Glass

That contract extension was a bomb exploding internally. It renewed my passion to win here in Kansas City. I especially wanted to do it for Mr. Glass and Dan for their show of support.

We didn't exactly get hot in 2010. That was the season we transitioned Alex Gordon to outfield and I had to make the tough decision to fire Trey Hillman, whom I replaced with Ned Yost. We lost 95 games and finished last in the Central.

OPERATION: FLIP THE SWITCH

Hanging on a wall in our house is a framed No. 35 Royals jersey. It's still stained with dirt from that May 6, 2011, game when the person who wore it, Eric Hosmer, made his highly anticipated major league debut.

A few weeks before that, Chino Cadahia, who joined the organization as a special assistant in 2011, and Jack Maloof, who was one of our hitting coaches who oversaw the development of all our young hitters, called and told me, "This guy [Hosmer] is ready for the major leagues. What are you waiting for?"

That seemed to be a common question. Gene Watson, our director of professional scouting, kept asking me, "When are we going to flip the switch?"

In other words, when were we going to start having fun and transitioning our talented minor league players to Kansas City?

Hos was the first one. He went hitless with two walks in that game on May 6, but he was ready. Hos ended up batting .293 with 19 home runs that season. Once he started hitting the ball — and he looked comfortable at first base — I knew we were close.

With Hosmer's success, the switch, indeed, had been flipped. About 10 days later, on May 18, Danny Duffy made his debut. A month after that, on June 10, it was Mike Moustakas' turn. August 10 marked the first game for Salvador Perez. And then Kelvin Herrera was a September

Shortly before we brought up Eric Hosmer and other talented minor league players in 2011, we used the term, "Operation: Flip the Switch." Three seasons later, Hos had some key hits for us during the 2014 postseason.

call-up, making his debut on September 21. That season, *Baseball America* rated our minor league system as the best in baseball.

A lot of thought goes into transitioning a player from the minors to the major leagues. Ideally you want them transitioning when there's positivity around the team, and the clubhouse is supportive. Most importantly, the manager and coaching staff need to be excited and believe the player can help the major league club. You don't want to transition young players to the major leagues if they're not going to play. But when it's all said and done, as I learned from one of my mentors, Bill Lajoie in Atlanta, you'd rather be a month too late than a month too early when advancing them to the major leagues. You want them hungry but to feel that they're deserving and prepared as much as they can be. *I'm ready for this next challenge*, should be their thought process.

As the young players were coming up, Gordo seemed to be comfortable in left field. He hit over .300 for the first time in his career (.303) with 23 home runs and 45 doubles, and he won his first Gold Glove.

By the way, at the bottom of that framed No. 35 jersey, which also includes two photos of Hos and the lineup cards, there's a plaque that reads:

OPERATION:
"FLIP THE SWITCH"
MAY 6, 2011
ERIC HOSMER'S MLB DEBUT

o o o

We lost 91 games in 2011, but I felt we were starting to turn the corner. I told Mr. Glass at our board meeting that December, "I expect us to keep getting better next season. However, in 2013, I don't know how we'll start but I think we'll finish strong. In 2014, we should compete from the first day to the last day."

At that time, I saw a young group of players we'd be able to settle in with. We went to spring training in 2012 with a clear vision of what our lineup would look like. It was young and talented with a lot of upside. We were able to sign Alex, Salvy, and Alcides Escobar to long-term deals. Even though he was supportive, Mr. Glass challenged me a great deal on these signings, as every owner would. There's always risk when you sign players to long-term deals because you worry about whether the player will remain hungry and if he will stay healthy over the length of the contract. Of course, two weeks later, Salvy hurt his knee. Talk about an endless pit in your stomach. I had to call Mr. Glass and tell him that Salvy was going to miss the first two months of the 2012 season. To Mr. Glass' credit, he was supportive and encouraged me to find somebody who could fill in until Salvy returned.

In 2012 we expected to be better, but we won only 72 games, primarily due to our pitching. We got Jeremy Guthrie in a trade with Colorado on July 20, but we needed more. We needed a top-of-the-rotation pitcher who could give us 200-plus innings. That led us to making what many consider to be one of the top two or three biggest trades in Royals history. If not monumental, it certainly was controversial.

THE TRADE

It takes two willing teams to make a trade. In August 2012, Tampa's general manager at the time, Andrew Friedman, and I began to discuss the needs of our teams. He knew we had interest in acquiring starting pitching, and we had an instinct they were going to move James Shields. That summer, their scouts were covering our minor league teams to see what we had in our system. When Major League Baseball's trade window opened, we began to craft the deal. Tampa was very interested in Wil Myers, but there was no way we were going to include him in the deal, so we left it at that. As they evaluated the market for Shields, Andrew and I continued to talk, but every time it came back to Shields for Wil.

Wil was a tremendous prospect. We drafted him in the third round out of high school in 2009. Scout Steve Connolly, who's now with Toronto, Junior Vizcaino, and J.J. Picollo wanted to sign Wil, but he was asking $2 million. I spoke with Dan Glass and explained to him the opinions of our scouts, and why we felt we needed this particular player. Oh, and by the way, we're going to give him $2 million and convert him to catcher. Ultimately, Dan and Mr. Glass trusted us and allowed us to go over budget to sign Myers. Two years later, many "experts" listed Wil as one of the top 10 prospects throughout the minor leagues. After the 2012 season he was a top five prospect. For our future, on the surface, it didn't make sense to trade that type of player.

The talks with Tampa heated up at the Winter Meetings, but I knew we weren't going to have a consensus in our organization. At the same time, we had homegrown talent on the field in Kansas City and we felt that if Alex, Billy,

Moose, Hos, Escobar, and Cain were going to become the productive players we envisioned, the team needed to play in meaningful games. That would help their focus and drive them to continue to improve and be great. Without making a deal that would drastically improve our rotation, though, we weren't going to be playing in meaningful games.

We continued to meet, but it was going nowhere. Very few people in our organization wanted to part with Wil Myers. There was a part of me that wanted to forget about it and move on. Any negotiation can become taxing mentally. Andrew and I both were frustrated during the process, but Gene Watson was instrumental in the discussions with Tampa and in keeping me motivated. There were plenty of reasons to do it and plenty not to.

We met that Tuesday night at the Winter Meetings, but it wasn't productive. We weren't getting anywhere. A few of our scouts were walking to the elevator in the hotel and ran into a Rays scout. One of our scouts said, "Look, if you guys want Wil Myers, you have to give us something. At least tell us what else you want." The Tampa scout said, "What I'll tell you is that we have four names on our list: Wil Myers, Jake Odorizzi, Mike Montgomery, and Patrick Leonard." That was it. Those scouts came back and told us. So Tim Conroy, one of our professional scouts, went in first and talked to Dayton about it. After he left, I went in to talk to Dayton. I said, "We need to do this. We never talked about four names. We know now what they want. These are four prospects. We have to win next year." Dayton asked what my point was. "You can't look at what you're giving up; you have to look at what you're getting. These guys are great talents but they're not going to help us win next year. We need to do this to take this organization to the next level."

—Gene Watson

Gene was right. If you focus on what you're giving up in a baseball trade, you'll rarely make the deal. Besides Wil, Jake Odorizzi was a tough pill to swallow because he's going to be a terrific pitcher. He'll be a perennial winner some day in the major leagues. So it's better to see how the players you're getting in return could impact your team. Shields had proven himself as a starter, capable of being our ace, and I felt Wade Davis could make a huge impact. There were people outside the organization who assumed that the trade was Shields for Myers and everyone else was a throw in. Wade Davis was not an add-on to the trade. As far as I was concerned, he could make a huge impact on our pitching staff. We felt that he could start. He had the pitches of a starting pitcher, he'd successfully started in the past, and we needed a starter. In 2012, he was dominant in the bullpen, so we knew that if it didn't work out as a starter, he could be a dominant reliever.

As we debated more about the trade, I pointed out to the others in the room that we had been instrumental in building farm systems in Atlanta and Philadelphia, and now, Kansas City. So we knew we could build a farm system. But it was time to prove that we could use that farm system to bring in talent to win at the major league level.

Our meeting went late into the night. I went to the white board and wrote down, by position, the names of every prospect we had in the system. The board was full of names. We had built a solid system. I took the four names — Myers, Odorizzi, Leonard, and Montgomery — off the board.

"Is this still a good system?" I asked. Everyone agreed that it still was a good system without those four players. We ended the meeting for the night.

I went back to my room, changed into some sweats, and then went back into Dayton's room. "We have to do this deal," I told him. "We need to give them the four names." Dayton agreed, so I called Rocco Baldelli, who was their assistant GM, and asked him to meet me in the hallway. When we were out there I said, "We've been given some information, so take these four names to Andrew. But I want to convey to you that you guys cannot go away from these four names. If you start digging for other names, this deal will be dead. It will be dead." That was Wednesday night, about 2:00 in the morning. The meetings ended without a deal. Sure enough, I find out that their scouts started calling our scouts, digging around. I was driving back home in Texas when Matt Arnold, Tampa's director of pro scouting, called me. I immediately told him, "Matt, it's not coming off these four names." As I was getting to Dallas, Dayton called and said the deal was done. Without that trade, I predicted that we would've won 74–78 games in 2013, and who knows if we're even around after the season. There's no question, in my mind, that was the single biggest trade the Royals ever made.

—Gene Watson

We knew we'd likely have Shields for only two years, but we were gearing toward being better in '13 and successful from day one to 162 in '14. If we don't make that deal, chances are we're going to get what we've always gotten. We had to have vision and aggressiveness, and then something good might happen. Sure enough, it did.

James brought a swagger and higher expectation level. He was all about winning and brought this philosophy to our entire clubhouse.

Like the trade that sent Zack Greinke to Milwaukee, this was a good baseball deal. Tampa got exactly what they were looking for and we got what we needed.

One of our best, yet most controversial, trades was when we acquired pitchers James Shields (No. 24) and Wade Davis (No. 22) from Tampa Bay on December 9, 2012.

2013

God's sense of humor continued—at least that seems like the best way to describe the 2013 season. Going into it, as I'd told Mr. Glass in 2011, I thought we'd finish strong even though I didn't know how we'd start.

Let's just say I wish we'd started better. The first month of the season was fine, as we went 14–10, but May was a disaster. It was so bad that on Monday night, May 27, *during* a game against St. Louis that started a four-game, home-and-home series, I'd had enough. We were 22–26 after losing five in a row and nine out of 10. I sent the following email—from my phone—to our top baseball operations leaders as a way to help keep them motivated and focused (not that they need it) going into the draft.

> As we prepare for draft day we must consume ourselves with players who are 100 percent passionate about baseball. They love it so much and want to be so great that they will concentrate the entire game EVERY GAME and work hard to make adjustments. They want to be so great that they love their teammates and want them to succeed above self. They want to be so great that they would never jeopardize their future greatness by abusing alcohol or drugs, infidelity, surrounding themselves with people of poor influence and spending too much time on hobbies that distract them from baseball. They manage their personal lives well! They play with innocence and would play for free. They respect all aspects of the game, especially diverse cultures, clubhouse environment, the travel, fans, and dealing with the media. I could go on forever but I'm sick of getting our asses kicked.
>
> We are going to fix this and make wiser decisions/interventions going forward. Let's have a great draft!
>
> Dayton

We ended up losing to St. Louis that night and the next two nights. During this stretch, I was reminded of a story that Christian Newsome, who's our pastor, told. Christian was a quarterback at Liberty University, playing for a great coach, Sam Rutigliano. Their team was going through a tough time, and Sam told his players this story: "Two men are in a boat in the ocean, and it takes on water. One man starts to pray, and the other man bails water. Who's right?" Sam looked around the room, while some guys muttered answers. Sam said, "They're both wrong. God wants them to do both—pray and bail." To me, that's validation for how you have to prepare and lead every day. You have to pray and ask God for wisdom. You have to ask him for influences in your life. God expects you to do your part. He's not going to just open doors and say, there you go.

After losing our third straight to the Cardinals and eight games in a row, I decided that we needed to make a change in hopes of turning things around. I'd had several conversations with George Brett in recent weeks about our offensive approach and lack of consistency with several players who had bright futures, especially Moose and Hos. Early in the losing streak, I called and asked him if he'd like to be our hitting coach. I've talked with George before every season about his role with the organization, because we want him to have as big of a role as he'd like, but the timing was never right. This time, for the first time, he didn't say no. We talked about it again a few days later. He said he'd talk to his wife Leslie about it. After the game on May 29, we talked again. George said he was ready to go. We agreed that we'd give it a month and reevaluate. I really felt, based on our previous conversations, that he was ready to commit full-time.

As I was watching one of the games right before going to St. Louis, Dayton called me, frustrated because we couldn't score runs. I told him they were swinging completely different from spring training. In spring training, guys were trying to make contact and put the ball in play. If you hit a double, fine. If you hit a triple, that's better. If you hit a home run, that's even better—but look for singles first. When the season started, it seemed like they were trying to hit home runs first and singles last. I was always told by Charley Lau that home runs come because of a good swing, not by trying to hit a home run. That's the one thing I tried to stress to the players. Hit the ball hard; don't try to hit it far. If you hit it hard, it's got a good chance of going far. But if you're trying to hit it far, your body becomes discombobulated at contact. That was the whole message from me—just do what you're capable of doing. I'd tell them, "Don't try to be someone else. Be the best player you can be. If you're the best player you can be, and Eric Hosmer is the best player he can be, and Alex Gordon's the best he can be, and so on, guess what—we're pretty good." If everyone's trying to do things they're not capable of doing, then nobody's going to be very good. And at that moment, the team wasn't good.

—George Brett

With one more game in St. Louis, we decided to meet the team on May 31 in Texas. I woke up early on the 30th on a stormy morning here in Kansas City, and I called George.

"What are you doing today?"

"Not much. I just finished working out."

"Let's get this done. I'll pick you up, and we'll drive to St. Louis."

I picked him up at 10:30 and we drove across Missouri to St. Louis. It was a tough day because we were reassigning hitting coaches Jack Maloof and Andre David. Jack and I have worked together since 2002, and Andre had done an unbelievable job. He was a very caring coach who always kept the morale high. As excited as I was for Jack and Andre and our organization when we hired them, I felt extremely disappointed for them on this May day. Ned Yost and I talked a lot leading up to the change about our trend offensively. We decided together that we needed to make a coaching change. He broke the news to Jack and Andre, who both were extremely gracious and understanding.

We talked to Pedro Grifol about working with George as a special assignment coach. Pedro would meet us in Texas.

After a press conference, George was in uniform that night. Ned and I addressed the team before the game. We thanked Jack and Andre for their time but said it was time to make a change and we needed a new voice as a hitting coach. George Brett was going to assume this position.

George then addressed the team.

There were so many expectations in 2013. It was going to be the year. Coming from my situation, I'd heard that before—"this is going to be our year"—and you start to put more pressure on yourself and the whole team. That's what we were going through in May. So when George came in, his personality is so outgoing that it was a perfect fit and a perfect time to put him in the dugout to help relax everyone. If there's someone that everyone around baseball, especially in our organization, respects, it's George Brett. He made a difference immediately. He delivered an incredible 15- to 20-minute pregame speech in the clubhouse that first night in St. Louis that fired us up. It was pretty passionate and inspirational. It would've gotten anyone ready to play. Without giving away too much, I'll just say the gist of it was that we didn't realize how good we were and how we didn't believe in ourselves. It was a confidence builder, and exactly what we needed. That was the start of us hitting our stride, which led to the success in 2014. The second half of 2013 helped us realize the importance of each game and how you can't take a game off. After that, everybody was ready to play every inning of every game.

—Alex Gordon

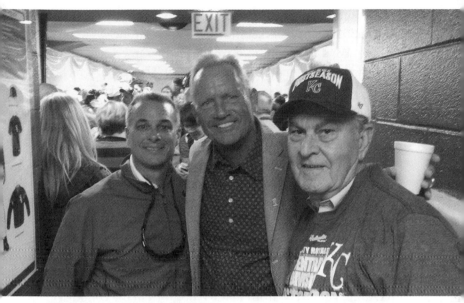

The night we clinched a playoff berth in Chicago on September 26, 2014, with George Brett, who was instrumental for us getting to that point, and David Glass, who showed incredible patience and support. *Photo courtesy of Jeff Davenport*

Among a lot of other things, I told them that when I played for the Royals, we expected to win every night when we took the field. We didn't hope to win; we expected to win. Going out there and hoping to win is different from expecting to win. I went on to tell them that when we went on the road, we wanted to step on the other team's throat. "That's what winners do," I said. "That's what good teams do. When they have someone down, they step on their throat and don't let them back up. Don't let them back in the game." I almost teared up talking about the organization and thinking about the confidence that Dayton had in me that he thought I could come in and help the team get better.

—George Brett

George's first night turned out to be somewhat precarious. Those hopes of finishing the season strong were on the line. We'd lost eight in a row and reassigned two outstanding baseball men earlier in the day. The game, which started an hour late because of rain, took a bad turn for us as the Cardinals scored two runs in the bottom of the first inning against Jeremy Guthrie. On the other side, our offense was lifeless against Michael Wacha, who was making his major league debut. He was absolutely shoving it.

Through an off-and-on rain, we trailed 2–1 until the top of the ninth, when Jeff Francoeur led off the inning with a home run. We scored two more runs in the inning on a double by Hosmer that scored Gordo and Escobar. And then, with no outs, the rain hammered us. While I sat in the suite at Busch Stadium, wondering what else could go wrong, I got a call from Peter Woodfork in the commissioner's office.

He explained the rule that since the Cardinals hadn't been able to hit in their half of the inning yet, and we took the lead in the top of the ninth, if the game were to get rained out, it would revert back to the eighth inning and we'd lose our ninth straight. Of course, next up for us was Texas, which was the hottest team in baseball then.

"We'll wait as long as we can," Peter assured me.

We kept waiting and waiting. The rains didn't seem to be letting up. I went down to the clubhouse to talk with Ned.

Peter called again. "We're not finishing the game."

"Peter, we need to play this game. We're not leaving until it's finished."

A few minutes later, Joe Torre, who's MLB's executive vice president of baseball operations, called me.

"Dayton, I don't see how we're going to get this in."

"Joe, we're looking at the radar right now in Ned's office. There's a small window of opportunity to play."

A few minutes later, Joe West, who's a great veteran umpire and cares about the integrity of the game, and was the crew chief that night, came to Ned's office. Initially he said we weren't going to be able to play, so we showed him the radar. The conditions weren't going to be great, but there was a small window.

Joe Torre called me back. "Dayton, we're going to bang the game."

"Joe, we can't bang this game. We've lost eight in a row, we replaced our hitting coaches earlier today, we're about to go to Texas, and we have a lead. We really need to figure out how to finish this game. We're not getting on the plane unless Mr. Glass calls me and says it's finished."

Joe was very calm and understood the situation. His main purpose is to uphold the integrity of the game. I respect him as much as anyone I've met in the game, but our purpose that night was to finish the game with a W. Joe said he'd look at it again. The next thing I know, Joe West was on the field with the umpiring crew, getting the St. Louis grounds crew to prepare the field. To their credit, the Cardinals grounds crew did an outstanding job.

Twelve minutes after the field was ready, at 3:14 AM, Greg Holland, in his toughness and competitiveness, threw a 1-2-3 inning, ending with Carlos Beltran grounding out. That was it. We snapped the eight-game losing streak by beating the Cardinals 4–2.

After losing three of the next four, we won six in a row and nine out of the next 10. That game in St. Louis put us on the path that led to a fantastic run in 2014. From that day forward, the team began to show a toughness and resiliency. We didn't have a losing month the rest of the season. Since that game in St. Louis to the end of the 2014 season, our team went 153–120.

Looking back, George Brett rescued us mentally. He did a terrific job, gave us a fresh start with renewed enthusiasm. George has a very natural way of communicating. I could sense that night that he had an influence. Obviously he was a great hitter, but he's also passionate about seeing the Kansas City Royals win.

George and Pedro really helped our hitters. For instance, I'd see them walking around the warning track with Moose and other players prior to batting practice. Obviously they were talking about their approach to hitting, while developing a relationship with the young players.

Pedro and I decided that one of our first goals was to turn around Mike Moustakas, who was struggling at the time. I called Mike and told him to be at the stadium at 4:00. He did and the three of us started off by taking about six laps around the stadium in Texas, just talking. I've known Mike since he signed, but Pedro didn't know him that well, so it was a chance for them to get to know each other better. We just talked about Mike's approach and philosophies. We did that with a few other guys who were struggling. The next thing you know, Pedro and Mike, for instance, were close. Mike developed so much faith in Pedro as a hitting coach that I think if Pedro would've told him that robbing a bank would help him as a hitter, Mike would've robbed a bank. It was a really good experience to be around Pedro and our players.

—George Brett

George's knowledge and passion rubbed off on the players. Embracing the past from our most recognizable player ever is a huge statement to our organization and players that George was willing to get out of his comfort zone, take that responsibility, and work for the organization. It was great to see him in a Royals uniform once again, even though it was only for six weeks.

o o o

We felt going into September that we had a chance for a wild-card spot. Certainly more hope than we've had since 2006.

The fun of September culminated on Sunday afternoon, the 22nd, our last home game. The energy in the city and at Kauffman Stadium was as high as it'd been since April 2009, in my experience. The environment in the ballpark was electric. It's funny how being in a pennant race helped things. The city came alive and showed that this is a great baseball town. We won the game on a walk-off grand slam by Justin Maxwell against Joakim Soria. I hated to see it against Soria, but as Rex Hudler would say, "It was a beautiful thing."

We played really well that last month, going 16–10, but Cleveland and Tampa Bay ended up getting the two wild-card spots. We were eliminated during the last week of the season. At that time, you start reflecting on games you could've won. Ultimately, that season taught our team a valuable lesson. Everything matters. If we could've just figured out how to get a couple more wins, probably in our disastrous 8–20 May, we might've been in the postseason. May was the difference. Everything matters.

IT "FEELS LIKE WE WON THE WORLD SERIES"

From the moment I arrived in Kansas City in the summer of 2006, one thing that I noticed and got aggravated with was seeing parents and grandparents walking into the stadium wearing Royals shirts with names like Brett, White, and Otis, while their kids and grandkids were wearing Red Sox and Yankees and Phillies shirts and jerseys with names like Pedroia, Jeter, and Howard. We had lost an entire generation of fans. We wanted to create a culture here that made kids want to wear blue shirts and jerseys with names like Gordon, Hosmer, Moustakas, and Perez. During the 2013 season, we started to see that shift, and it was obvious that our fans were embracing this group of players. And it was wonderful.

During our annual postseason press conference, writer Jeffrey Flanagan asked me about my future in Kansas City. As I was answering I remarked, "A part of me feels like we won the World Series." Everyone in that room knew what I meant, but you would've thought I just said that we were going to sign Elvis Presley in hopes of winning the World Series. (Actually, that statement might've been received better than the one I made.)

My answer, which was truthful then and I stick with it now, simply meant that for how our season went, how we'd battled back from that horrible May, how we were in the hunt for a postseason spot until the last week, and by doing all of that, our environment was changing. Fans were coming back. Our players were enjoying the community.

I know what it's like to win a World Series; I was a part of one in Atlanta. But to be in a pennant race in late September, and see the environment at the K changing because of our players and the way they went out and competed each night was an incredible feeling. The excitement around baseball in Kansas City was unmatched. People cared. The excitement in the stadium was electric. Our television ratings shot up to the highest level in our franchise's history. Fans in all phases of their lives fell in love with this team. Amateur players were on fields throughout our community emulating Hosmer, Moustakas, and Gordon. And we started seeing young fans showing up at the K wearing shirts with names such as Shields, Holland, and Perez. Baseball was back.

Yes, I know how it feels to win a World Series. Indeed. God has a sense of humor. As one of my Christian mentors, Tim Cash, once told me once, "It's better to be persecuted for who you are than praised for who you're not."

CHAPTER 10
THE PROCESS COMES TO FRUITION

HEADING INTO THE 2014 SEASON, after the way we finished 2013, we felt the key pieces were in place on the field and in the dugout. Returning to Ned Yost's coaching staff were Rusty Kuntz, Pedro Grifol, Dave Eiland, and Doug Henry. Pedro, whom I've admired for a long time because of his intelligence as a baseball man, had a great reputation as a farm director in Seattle. Dave Eiland, who was starting his third season as pitching coach, has done a tremendous job of keeping our pitchers focused and preparing them to win. And, of course, Doug Henry, who's our bullpen coach, keeps that very talented group focused and ready to perform. We had three new additions to our coaching staff: Mike Jirschele, Don Wakamatsu, and Dale Sveum. They were obviously going to impact our coaching staff and our team in a very positive way. Wak is a great thinker, poised, and extremely prepared, and I have tremendous respect for Dale as a teacher with a tough, no-nonsense approach. He's never afraid to put his relationship on the line with a player. It's a wonderful honor and privilege to work with these men.

We liked our roster, but over 162 games adjustments always have to be made. As I told our owner, David Glass, a couple years earlier, I thought 2014 was the season we'd compete from the first day until the last.

We didn't expect it to be all rosy, and it wasn't. In fact, during spring training, Luke Hochevar hurt his elbow and would require Tommy John surgery. He was done before the season began. We were counting on him as a big part of our bullpen. In 2013 he went 5–2 with a 1.92 ERA and 82 strikeouts in 70 1/3 innings.

As Ned and I discussed it, we decided that our best option would be moving Wade Davis into Hoch's spot. No one — and I mean no one — could've predicted how dominant Wade would be. He was nearly perfect for the entire season. He didn't allow an extra-base hit for 43 appearances and didn't allow a run for 20 appearances.

The back end of our bullpen with Kelvin Herrera, Davis, and Greg Holland was the most dominant trio of relief pitchers I've ever seen. They were as impressive to watch as the Maddux Glavine Smoltz trio was.

o o o

In mid-June, we went into first place after beating Detroit 11–4. That was our ninth win in a row and 10th in our previous 11 games. Everything was clicking. At 38–32, we hadn't reached the halfway point of the season yet. There was still plenty of baseball to be played.

At the end of that month, we made one of the biggest signings of the past few years, when we added veteran outfielder Raul Ibanez. I've always liked the way he played the game. It's obvious he has great passion to play, and he's regarded as one of the best leaders in baseball.

As we were slipping in the standings, I felt that signing Raul, who'd been released by the Angels on June 21, would improve our club. He did improve it, but not in the way most people would've expected. After all, he hit only .188 in 33 games during the rest of the year.

Raul's impact was felt shortly after the All-Star break. In late July we went on a stretch where we won three out of 13 games. We were slipping badly in the division, as Boston swept us and we were beginning an important series in Chicago. Being the 19-year veteran that he was, Raul called a players-only meeting.

> *We started to hit our stride for 2014 in May 2013. Everyone in the clubhouse expected that to continue in 2014, but right after the All-Star break the Red Sox swept us in Boston. We had gone from leading the Central Division in mid-June to third place and seven games back a month later. To put it mildly we were down and not feeling good about ourselves at all. After Boston we went to Chicago and lost the first game there. We had a players-only meeting, and Raul Ibanez, who'd joined the club at the end of June, gave an incredible pregame speech. Basically, he pointed out to every player that we didn't realize how good we are, and how, coming from another team previously, he knew that teams feared coming to Kauffman to play us. Coming from a guy like that, who'd been in the majors for 20 years, it picked us up. The rest is history.*
>
> *—Alex Gordon*

Without a doubt, the rest was history. That was the turning point. From that moment, our players finished with a 41–23 record.

The season ultimately became successful for us as an organization on September 26 in Chicago. That night, with many of our front-office people in the stands at U.S. Cellular Field, the Royals beat the White Sox and clinched a postseason berth for the first time in 29 years.

THREE TYPES OF PLAYERS

Like all of us in life, baseball players go through different stages and levels of maturity throughout their careers. Closely observing players since 1994, when it comes to their makeup, players fit into three main categories: fearful, overcomer, and fearless. A player can be in any of these stages at any time during his career. Ultimately, it comes down to accountability and being focused on being a great teammate. If the team is going to reach its ceiling, the best players have to be the best competitors, work the hardest, and care the most. After joining our club in late June, Raul Ibanez's influence was instrumental in helping our 2014 club, as a group, go from overcomers to fearless on their way to the American League championship.

The Fearful Player: This player won't trust the development process. He's a poor self-evaluator. He blames his coaches and teammates for his failures. He's insecure about where he was taken in the draft. He can be uncomfortable with baseball's diverse cultures, and he's always making excuses. He's consumed with self, and doesn't know how to be a teammate. Because of the importance of being able to manage failure, his spirit will eventually be crushed. Even the player who Jim Beauchamp, one of my mentors, would call "chosen" ends up being miserable later in his career and throughout his life. It's not about the team. There are plenty of examples of talented, producing major league players who are in the "fearful" stage. They put up great numbers, but their teammates and coaches don't respect them because it's all about self. It's difficult for teams to win championships with players who possess these traits because they bring the team down.

The Overcomer: This player is starting to understand what accountability is and trusting the development process, physically and mentally. He is outlining what type of player he needs to be and adopting

continued

a team-first mentality. The player is becoming an honest self-evaluator because he knows this is the only way he can improve. Hopefully he is overcoming his fearfulness while his skill and health as a baseball player remain.

The Fearless Player: This player is a great teammate. He does whatever needs to be done to help the team win. He never lets a situation, a circumstance, or an event drive a wedge between him and what he loves to do. He especially doesn't let the circumstance or situation affect the team. He understands that everyone's success is tied together. He's accountable; he doesn't make excuses. He answers the media's tough questions. He is completely focused on what he has to do to prepare and give his best for the team each day. The bottom line: he plays for something bigger than himself.

I can find success in nearly any season, but that night in Chicago, more than a generation of monkeys flew off our backs. At that moment, although our overall goal — as it is each year with every major league club — was to win the World Series, we reached that initial stepping stone of the postseason.

THE POSTSEASON

My reaction to the postseason contests is below. The italicized game recaps are taken from *Out of the Blue*, Matt Fulks' book commemorating the Royals' 2014 season.

Wild-Card Game—Royals 9, A's 8 (12 innings)

Well, that was fast. Or so it seemed. Twenty-nine years of waiting, of frustration, of thinking every spring, "Maybe this is our year," to the mid-summer realization, "There's always next year." After 29 years the Royals were finally here, the postseason, and in less than 29 minutes—or however long it took Oakland to put together a five-run sixth inning—it was over. This time of the year teams don't come back from 7–3 deficits after seven innings, especially a team like Kansas City that had spent so much energy during the roller-coaster 2014 season just to reach the postseason.

But in front of a rocking, standing-room-only crowd of 40,502 at Kauffman Stadium, the young and inexperienced Royals were brought back to life in the wildest of wild-card games. . . . Pitcher Jon Lester, whom Oakland acquired at the trade deadline for an anticipated postseason run, held a comfortable 7–3 lead. Bad news for the Royals, considering Lester has had Kansas City's number throughout his career,

The pure joy and childlike excitement that is showing on everyone's faces after Christian Colon (with helmet) scored the winning run in the 12th inning of the wild-card game against Oakland is one of the many reasons I love this game.

regardless of the team name on his uniform. In fact, Lester, who was 4–0 against the Royals in 2014, shut out Kansas City in Boston on July 20, and then two starts later, on August 2—his first appearance for the A's—he beat the Royals again.

Salvador Perez, who looked silly throughout the game at the plate, reached out for a low-and-away pitch with two strikes and pulled the ball past diving third baseman Josh Donaldson. Christian Colon, who has good speed, scored easily, giving the Royals a walk-off win—their first postseason victory since Game 7 of the 1985 World Series.

I was in our baseball operations suite, watching the game alone. When you're down by four runs to a pitcher who not only had great success against your team, but embarrassed them with a no-hitter a few years earlier, the natural thought is *Uh-oh*. But I tried to stay optimistic and just kept thinking, if we could get base runners we could win. Sure enough, that's what happened.

In extra innings, Donnie Williams, who broke me in as a scout in 1994 and is now one of my senior advisors, came down to the suite, and we watched the end of the game together. That was a cool moment.

I need to add that the crowd that night at Kauffman Stadium was made up of the most incredible and most electric fans that I'd seen in our stadium. That was an amazing night that started an unbelievable journey for the next month.

ALDS: Game 1—Royals 3, Angels 2 (11 innings)

Two nights after beating the A's in 12 innings, the Royals used extra frames again, this time to beat the Angels 3–2 in 11 innings.

In the top of the 11th, with the scored tied 2–2, the No. 9 hitter, Mike Moustakas, a Los Angeles native, belted a 374-foot home run to right field that reached the elevated seats off reliever Fernando Salas and gave Kansas City a 3–2 lead.

The Angels had tied the game (at 2–2) in the bottom of the fifth when David

Freese led off with a homer to left off Kansas City's surprise starter Jason Vargas, who was 1–5 in his last six starts and hadn't won since September 3. Against his former Angels mates, Vargas looked more like the pitcher who had ended April with a 2.40 ERA. He gave up three hits and two runs—both on solo home runs—in six innings.

There were people who were surprised about Jason Vargas starting Game 1 of the ALDS. We felt that Vargy would go out, with extra focus against his old team in his old home stadium, and get back to the Jason Vargas that we saw earlier in the season. Sure enough, he did. We had been tracking Vargy for three years. We liked him because of his command of the fastball on both sides of the plate and his conviction in his change-up. We knew he'd be a great fit in our ballpark with our spectacular defense.

ALDS: Game 2—Royals 4, Angels 1 (11 innings)

For a third consecutive game, the Royals went into extra innings. For the third consecutive game, they won. For a third consecutive game, it was a homegrown player who came through in the clutch.

With Game 2 of the ALDS tied at 1–1 in the top of the 11th after Lorenzo Cain beat out an infield single, Eric Hosmer launched a 399-foot homer to right with a picture-perfect swing at Angel Stadium of Anaheim. It was Hosmer's third hit of the game. Later in the inning, Alex Gordon, who knocked in Kansas City's first run back in the second inning, scored on a base hit by Salvador Perez, giving the Royals their eventual 4–1 win.

The streak, which Hollywood would turn down as too unbelievable, started in the wild-card game when Perez, who signed as an undrafted free agent in 2006, nearly four months after Dayton Moore became general manager, knocked in Christian Colon in the 12th inning in Kansas City. It continued in Game 1 of the ALDS, when Mike Moustakas, the Royals' first-round pick (second overall) in 2007, launched an 11th-inning home run against the Angels. The blast by Hosmer, Kansas City's first-round pick (third overall) in 2008, gave the Royals a 2–0 lead in the series.

It's interesting and somewhat fun to read those paragraphs because of three of the names mentioned: Eric Hosmer, Mike Moustakas, and Salvador Perez. All three of those players came up in the same season, all three are expected to continue to contribute to our team's success, and all three made big contributions during the postseason.

ALDS: Game 3—Royals 8, Angels 3

In front of another rambunctious standing-room crowd (40,657) at Kauffman Stadium, the Royals rested the extra-inning drama for a game as they jumped on Angels starter C.J. Wilson early en route to an 8–3 win and three-game sweep of the Angels in the American League Division Series.

Trailing 1–0 after a Mike Trout home run—his first hit of the series—the Royals got three runs in the bottom of the first thanks to a bases-loaded double by Alex Gordon that scored Nori Aoki, Lorenzo Cain, and Billy Butler, and gave Kansas City a 3–1 lead. That hit also knocked Wilson out of the game after two-thirds of an inning.

The Royals put the game out of reach in the third when Eric Hosmer hit his second home run of the ALDS—a 427-foot bomb to center—that put the Royals ahead 5–1.

In 1996, while I was with the Braves, we beat the Yankees in the first two games of the World Series in New York but then lost the next three in Atlanta. When you win two in New York and you're coming home, you feel pretty good about your chances. I kept that memory, and felt the same way when we came back from Los Angeles in the ALDS. Even though we were coming home, we knew the Angels were extremely talented—the American League's best team. We didn't want to give them any momentum. That was one of the most enjoyable games I've ever been a part of. For Gordo to drive the ball to the alley in the first in a great at-bat really showed his fight, grit, and determination. He has an incredible desire to win, regardless of what happens. He was the right guy to be in that spot—you had a feeling he'd have a great at-bat, even though C.J. Wilson is a tough lefty. We rolled after Gordo's hit. We played as good a game as we could. I'll never forget celebrating the moments of that game together.

ALCS: Game 1—Royals 8, Orioles 6 (10 innings)

Ask Mike Moustakas—the author of an extra-inning home run in Game 1 of the American League Division Series—if he's one of the leaders of this team, and he'll deflect the question and point to Alex Gordon.

"He's our backbone," Moustakas said. "He's our heart and soul. He's our leader."

Gordon, the Royals Gold Glove left fielder carried the Royals on his back in Game 1 of the American League Championship Series in Baltimore.

In yet another extra-inning affair—the fourth in five games for the Royals— Gordon had a dramatic George Brett-esque night for Kansas City. An at-bat after being plunked in the neck by Andrew Miller, Gordon launched a leadoff home run off Darren O'Day into the dark Baltimore sky in the 10th inning that put the Royals ahead 6–5. For good measure, three batters later, Moustakas added a two-run homer. It's a good thing. The Orioles scored a run in the bottom of the inning, making the final 8–6 in favor of the Royals.

As you've likely figured out already, I could continue writing about Alex Gordon and his importance to this franchise. His performance in Game 1 of the ALCS, though, will go down as one of the best single performances in Royals postseason history.

ALCS: Game 2—Royals 6, Orioles 4

Lorenzo Cain's wife, Jenny, gave birth to the couple's first baby, Cameron Loe, three days before the ALCS began. Four days later, daddy put on a performance that Cameron will one day tell his kids about.

Cain, who was on base four times and scored two runs in Game 1, went 4-for-5 with two runs and an RBI in Kansas City's 6–4 win in Game 2 of the ALCS at Camden Yards. Cain joins George Brett as the only Royals with four hits in a postseason game. (Brett did it twice.) Adding to Cain's day at the plate, he made two more outstanding plays in the outfield.

When we made the Zack Greinke trade with Milwaukee that included Cain, he'd had just a small taste of the major leagues. Many people felt he was major league ready, but we sent him to the minor leagues. He didn't complain at all, but I could tell he wasn't sure what to think of us, and we had to build that relationship. To see him on that stage throughout the postseason and to know what he meant to our team in 2014 was incredible. I was happy and proud for him in his personal growth as a player and as a man. He developed a lot of trust with the organization. He obviously went on to have an unbelievable ALCS, not only Game 2. So it was very special, a few nights later, seeing him hold up the American League Championship Series MVP trophy. And for him to be holding up that trophy wearing an infectious smile, with his wife, Jenny, and their newborn son, Cameron Loe, just a few feet away, is something Lorenzo will never forget. I don't think Royals fans will, either.

ALCS: Game 3—Royals 2, Orioles 1

Due to rain, the Royals had to wait an extra day to see if they could continue their undefeated postseason streak. Whether it was the weather or the late-night games leading up to the Tuesday night Game 3 contest against Baltimore, the Kauffman Stadium crowd seemed tame. They certainly were more subdued than in the two earlier postseason games against the A's and Angels.

That all changed in the top of the sixth inning against the Orioles. With the scored tied 1–1 and Jason Frasor relieving starting pitcher Jeremy Guthrie, Baltimore's

THE PROCESS COMES TO FRUITION

Adam Jones popped a ball in foul territory beyond third base. Although it looked as if it was headed for the seats, Mike Moustakas tracked it the whole way and, as the wind pushed it back over the dugout, reached out and flipped into the dugout suite as he made the catch.

And then it happened. As if snapping out of a daydream, Kauffman Stadium became electric again with chants of "Let's go, Royals!" ringing from the crowd of 40,183.

Frasor ended up pitching a perfect sixth. The crowd remained in a frenzy in the bottom half of the inning when, with Jarrod Dyson on third, Billy Butler lifted a sacrifice fly to deep left that broke the tie and gave Kansas City a 2–1 lead. That's how the score would stand as the Royals took a three-games-to-none lead.

This catch by Mike Moustakas will be on postseason highlight reels for years to come. More importantly, Moose's catch in the sixth inning of Game 3 against Baltimore reignited our crowd as we went on to take a three-games-to-none lead in the ALCS.

Moose displayed a tremendous amount of personal growth during the 2014 season. We made the necessary decision in May to send him down to Triple A Omaha. He was struggling in Kansas City, batting just .152 during the early part of the season. We talked to Moose about it, but he's a good self-evaluator. Players never want to be demoted to the minors, but Mike knew there were some areas where he needed to improve, and I felt Omaha was going to be the best situation for him. He has a very good rapport with minor league hitting coach Tommy Gregg. I knew Tommy and Mike would make positive strides in getting Mike back to the major leagues. Sure enough, although he didn't tear things up, when he came back, without question he had some big moments throughout the postseason. That catch over the dugout suites did ignite the crowd. That will go down as one of those catches you see on highlight reels for years to come.

ALCS: Game 4—Royals 2, Orioles 1

The Royals organization—including its fans—had been waiting 29 years for this moment. They didn't let it pass one more day. Kansas City jumped ahead of Baltimore with two runs in the bottom of the first inning on a chamber of commerce Wednesday afternoon, and went on to beat the Orioles 2–1, clinching the American League title for the first time since 1985 and just the third time in the organization's history.

In the process, the Royals became the first team to start a postseason with eight consecutive wins. Perhaps more shockingly to some—at least to the haters—manager Ned Yost became the first skipper in major league history to win his first eight postseason games.

So many images from after that game will be burned into my mind for the rest of my life. There was the way we scored in the first inning, Gordo's catch against the fence in left field, the trophy presentation afterward. For me, though, it was being able to spend time after the game with my family. I was able to take Marianne and our kids to the clubhouse and let them meet with the families of our front office. That was special. When you're in this business, families have to make a lot of sacrifices. Going down to the clubhouse with all of our families was the perfect way to thank them.

One image that will remain vivid for me from the 2014 postseason will be Lorenzo Cain (left) proudly holding up the well-deserved MVP trophy after the ALCS. While on the stage (below), I was overwhelmed with emotion.

WS: Game 1—Giants 7, Royals 1

Heading into the World Series, James Shields was 1–0 in three postseason starts for the Royals in 2014 with a 5.64 ERA. In those three starts, his longest outing was six innings against the Angels. The other two games were five innings apiece against Oakland and Baltimore. Before Game 1 of the World Series, Shields downplayed the numbers and revealed that he passed a kidney stone during the ALCS. Royals manager Ned Yost gave Shields a vote of confidence, pointing out how much Shields wanted to put his AL playoff games behind him.

Someone forgot to alert the San Francisco Giants, who spoiled the feel-good story of the Royals and snapped Kansas City's 11-game postseason winning streak (dating back to 1985) on the opening night of the World Series at Kauffman Stadium.

As with Game 4 against Baltimore, this game was special because of something personal. Many people don't realize this, but John Schuerholz, in supporting me, our staff, and our organization, took time out of his hectic schedule to be with us in Kansas City for that first game. It was special for me to be able to spend that moment with him.

The last time the Royals played in a World Series game, I was the general manager, so I thought it was only appropriate to be there. Dayton and his staff took good care of me; it was a delight. It was the worst game the Royals had played in months, but given the circumstances, their opponent, and the pitcher they faced, it's understandable. The postseason was validation for the plan they put in place, how they worked the plan, and their willingness to be patient. One key was the support that Mr. Glass showed them. I know how thrilled he was. Dayton and his staff did a great job of putting the right mix of players together, which was reflected in the run they put on in the latter part of the year and getting to the World Series. They played extremely well.

—John Schuerholz

HOMEGROWN WORLD SERIES

When I became general manager in June 2006, I told anyone who'd listen that in order to compete in this market, the majority of our roster needed to be made up of "homegrown" players. Looking at our 25-man World Series roster, we drafted or signed as non-drafted free agents 12 players. Four players were acquired in trades for players in our farm system.

Drafted or signed as a non-drafted free agent:

- Billy Butler—First-round draft pick in 2004
- Alex Gordon—First-round draft pick in 2005
- Jarrod Dyson—50th-round pick in 2006
- Salvador Perez—Signed as non-drafted free agent in 2006
- Kelvin Herrera—Signed as a non-drafted free agent in 2006
- Mike Moustakas—First-round draft pick in 2007
- Danny Duffy—Third-round draft pick in 2007
- Greg Holland—10th-round draft pick in 2007
- Eric Hosmer—First-round draft pick In 2008
- Yordano Ventura—Signed as a non-drafted free agent in 2008
- Terrance Gore—20th-round draft pick in 2011
- Brandon Finnegan—First-round draft pick in 2014

Players acquired by using prospects from our farm system:

- Lorenzo Cain/Alcides Escobar—Acquired from Milwaukee in a December 2010 trade for our 2002 first-round pick, Zack Greinke. Part of that trade included us getting pitcher Jake Odorizzi.
- Wade Davis/James Shields—Acquired from Tampa Bay in December 2012 for four players, including Wil Myers (third-round draft pick in 2009), Mike Montgomery (first-round draft pick in 2008), Patrick Leonard (fifth-round pick in 2011), and Odorizzi.

Hall of Fame scout and mentor Paul Snyder and his wife, Petie, came to Kansas City for the first two games of the World Series. Paul taught me so many lessons about this business and about life while I worked with him in Atlanta. Those invaluable lessons have been applied to the way we operate in Kansas City. So, as it was with John being in Kansas City, it was special for me to share this postseason moment with Paul.

WS: Game 2—Royals 7, Giants 2

The chant started raining down from the Kauffman Stadium crowd of 40,446: "Billy Butler..." Clap, clap... clap, clap, clap. "Billy Butler..." Clap, clap... clap, clap, clap. "Billy Butler..." Clap, clap... clap, clap, clap.

Finally, at the, um, encouragement of others in the dugout, Butler went up a couple steps and tipped his cap.

Usually a curtain call is reserved for a big home run late in the game or an outstanding pitching performance. Butler's tip of the cap came in the sixth inning. After a base hit. Well, maybe a little more important than just a base hit. With the game tied at 2–2, San Francisco starting pitcher Jake Peavy gave up a base hit to Lorenzo Cain and then walked Eric Hosmer. As Butler, who has hit Peavy well throughout his career, waited on deck, Giants manager Bruce Bochy went to his bullpen and brought in Jean Machi. Butler greeted him with the RBI single that scored Cain and gave the Royals a 3–2 lead. Royals manager Ned Yost sent in Terrance Gore to run for Butler. And the chanting began.

Billy had been struggling up to this point in the postseason, but his presence in our lineup was very important. He carried us numerous times in the past. It was gratifying to see him come up with a big hit in our organization's first World Series win since Game 7 in 1985.

WS: Game 3—Royals 3, Giants 2

Jeremy Guthrie had pitched in 275 regular-season games and one postseason contest during his 11-year major league career. Tim Hudson had pitched in 458

THE PROCESS COMES TO FRUITION

regular-season games and 12 postseason games during a 16-year career. Neither had made a World Series appearance. That changed for both in the best pitching duel the Royals have had during this postseason.

But it'll be the 35-year-old Guthrie who'll never forget the night of October 24, 2014—the night he pitched one of the best games of his career and helped the Royals take a two-games-to-one lead over San Francisco as the Royals beat the Giants 3–2 at AT&T Park.

Guthrie gave up two runs and four hits over five innings. He didn't allow any walks or strike out any. Hudson, 39, went 5 2/3 innings, giving up three runs and four hits. He struck out two and walked one. Guthrie retired 10 in a row from the last out in the second until Brandon Crawford opened the sixth with a base hit. Hudson retired 11 in a row from the last out in the second until Alcides Escobar singled with one out in the sixth. During one stretch the two pitchers combined for 20 consecutive outs.

Before we acquired Guthrie on July 20, 2012, we were attracted to him because of his career path, and how he'd persevered. He was a first-round pick out of college by Cleveland in 2002, but in his first three years with the Indians he made 16 appearances and had a 6.08 ERA, so he was viewed as a bust. But he kept working and overcoming. We actually tried to trade for him when he was with Baltimore, but we couldn't execute a deal. So in 2012, while he was struggling with Colorado, we acquired him in exchange for Jonathan Sanchez, who was struggling at the time for us. Although Guth was going to be a free agent after the season, the deal seemed like a no-brainer.

When I discussed it beforehand with team president Dan Glass, he said he'd support our decision, even though this was going to cost us $1 million at a time when we weren't moving up in the standings and we were losing financially.

He just said, "I'll support you if you think it'll work."

"Dan, he's definitely an upgrade over Jonathan," I replied. "This move improves our rotation and gives us a chance to develop a relationship with Jeremy."

As it turned out, we got exactly what we expected with Guthrie. After going 3–9 with a 6.35 ERA with the Rockies, he went 5–3 with a 3.16 ERA for us and confirmed what we believed already: he's prepared, he's smart, he competes, and most importantly he throws strikes. Through the last two months of the 2012 season, we exhibited to him that we were trying to build something special in Kansas City, so after the season, he re-signed with us as a free agent. He won a career-high 15 games in 2013 and 13 games in 2014. In the postseason, it was special to see Guth's perseverance pay off by reaching the postseason, beating one of his former teams, Baltimore, in the ALCS, and then winning his first World Series appearance.

WS: Game 4—Giants 11, Royals 4

Royals manager Ned Yost has answered questions until his face turned blue throughout this postseason about the comfort level of getting a game to the seventh inning with a lead or a tie and then turning the ball over to the unbeatable bullpen.

He and the Royals came up an inning short in Game 4 as the bullpen not named Herrera, Davis, and Holland was beatable—and, boy was it ever—in an 11–4 San Francisco win Saturday night at AT&T Park. The series is now tied at 2–2, which guarantees a return to Kansas City.

This is the one postseason game that makes me cringe. I thought we had a pretty good chance of winning this one. You have to give the San Francisco hitters credit for scoring against our talented bullpen. If we'd taken a 3–1 lead in the series, needing one more win with two more games in front of our fans at the K, there's little doubt in my mind that we would've won the World Series.

WS: Game 5—Giants 5, Royals 0

James Shields needed to bounce back and pitch his best game of the postseason. For all intents and purposes, he did what he needed to do to win.

Of course, though, the Royals knew this would be a tall order, beating Giants ace Madison Bumgarner, even with Shields. Not just because Bumgarner cruised to a win in Game 1 of this World Series against Shields, but largely because Bumgarner, in spite of not getting the national attention until now, is proving to be one of the best pitchers in World Series history.

Unfortunately for the Royals and their hopes of heading home with a 3–2 lead in the World Series, Bumgarner cemented his name alongside the game's greats with a complete-game, 5–0 shutout of Kansas City at AT&T Park, giving San Francisco that 3–2 lead in the World Series.

James Shields didn't have a great postseason and was criticized because of his nickname "Big Game James," but he was a huge reason we were in the postseason. He did exactly what we wanted and expected when he came from Tampa. He brought a swagger that was invaluable for our young players to see.

WS: Game 6—Royals 10, Giants 0

Perhaps we need to start calling Royals manager Ned Yost "Yostradamus" after the way things have been going for Kansas City during the last couple games of the World Series. Yost has commented several times about how, deep down, he's been hoping for this World Series to go seven games. He also showed unwavering confidence in his club after Madison Bumgarner and the Giants forced the Royals into an elimination Game 6.

Well, Yostradamus, you were correct. In front of another rambunctious Kauffman Stadium crowd, the Royals made beating the Giants look easy in a 10–0 win in Game 6, bringing about Wednesday night's Game 7—a winner-take-all end to the major league season.

The way they got through the Giants in Game 6 may matter. Behind another strong pitching performance from future staff ace but current rookie Yordano Ventura, the Royals put the game out of reach with a seven-run second inning. Mike Moustakas gave Kansas City the lead with a double off starter Jake Peavy just inside the first-base bag that scored Alex Gordon, who led off the inning with a single and moved to third on a base hit by Salvador Perez. After Omar Infante struck out with runners at second and third, Alcides Escobar turned in the play of the game. He knocked a slow roller toward first. Giants first baseman Brandon Belt fielded the ball but hesitated, making sure Perez wasn't headed home. By the time Belt decided to make the play at first, Escobar had scooted by him and slid safely, feet first, into the bag. Nori Aoki then ripped an RBI single to left that gave Kansas City a 2–0 lead and ended Peavy's night.

That was just a great game with a lot of players contributing, starting with pitcher Yordano Ventura. After winning that game, we had momentum going into Game 7, especially at home. This has been debated, but there can be momentum from game to game, at least early in the next game. Longtime Baltimore manager Earl Weaver was asked about momentum one time, and he answered, "Momentum is the next day's starting pitcher." I agree wholeheartedly. After I'm finished thinking about that night's game, I start thinking about our next day's starter, the overall pitching matchup with the other team, and the status of our bullpen. Leaving the ballpark after Game 6 of the 2014 World Series, I felt good because we had Jeremy Guthrie starting for us, and our bullpen had been lights-out all season. We knew Guth would embrace the challenge, throw strikes, and compete. He had done that throughout his career.

I'm sure the feelings I had about our club heading into the game were similar to what John Schuerholz felt about the Royals in Game 7 in 1985. That Royals team had momentum against St. Louis after two consecutive wins, including a dramatic Game 6 victory.

WS: Game 7—Giants 3, Royals 2

Ninety feet. That's all that separated the Royals from pulling off the improbable in the same place where this crazy journey started 29 days ago. For a brief moment in late September, it would've been more plausible to find Elvis eating a North Town Burger at Chappell's than it would be to even imagine the Royals getting past the wild-card game, let alone reaching the World Series.

And yet, here they were, 90 feet—just 30 yards—from tying Game 7 with two outs in the bottom of the ninth inning with arguably the greatest pitcher in World Series history facing the Royals player who had came up big in a similar spot 29 days earlier.

After two innocent outs in the bottom of the ninth with a strikeout by Eric Hosmer and a foul pop out to first by Billy Butler, Alex Gordon, who had an RBI double in the second inning, stood at the plate against Giants ace Madison Bumgarner. Three days ago, Bumgarner mowed down the Royals for the second time in this World Series in a complete-game, four-hit shutout. Now he was one out from getting a five-inning save while allowing no runs and only one hit.

Gordon kept Kansas City's hopes alive, though, as he lined Bumgarner's 87 mph slider to left-center. Center fielder Gregor Blanco misplayed the ball, and it rolled to the wall. Left fielder Juan Perez had trouble grabbing the ball, which allowed Gordon to motor into third base. In the aftermath, some fans wished third-base coach Mike Jirschele would've sent Gordon home. (Even an average throw from shortstop Brandon Crawford likely would've nailed Gordon by 27 feet for the final out of the Series.) Either way, he stood at third with two outs and Salvador Perez at the plate. . . . Bumgarner decided to throw Perez high fastballs, which are the easiest to see and hardest to hit. Bumgarner threw six pitches to Perez, all fastballs. Perez popped up the last one in foul territory, near the Giants dugout at third base. Pablo Sandoval camped under it and made the catch. The Giants, 3–2 winners in the game, had won their third World Series title in five years.

I knew perspective would take over as it always does, but the first 48 hours after the game were especially tough. It felt as if someone ripped out my heart. I thought we matched up well with the Giants and could win. Our players competed so well and fearlessly. Losing was very disappointing.

> *I knew we'd get here, the only question was when. But it was worth the wait—what a great ride! Everything happened so fast. There are so many responsibilities with guests and other things that occupy your time during the games that suddenly it's over and you wish you'd enjoyed it more. But it's about as much fun as I've ever had in an October. I'd do it all over again in a heartbeat.*
>
> *—David Glass*

IT'S MORE THAN A SEASON

A career in baseball leaves a lot of scars on your heart. A few days after Game 7, we began to focus on the prospect of doing it all over again. What do we need to do to get back? What players will we lose and who can we get? Every team will change the next season and the season after that and the season after that. The ways to attack opponents and match up with them changes each year.

As in life, we have to learn from this and get better each day. We have a great stable of inspirational leaders in our baseball operations department and throughout our organization. Inspirational leaders have the ability to speak with authority. They have in-depth knowledge and can communicate this knowledge in a very passionate way. This style is convincing, but I believe it's extremely difficult to motivate others by words alone. Leaders must take action, prepare, and prove that they will sacrifice for the team. Taking time to study, appreciate, and know the history of your organization shows respect and that you are deeply committed. I can't imagine any player not wanting to play here in Kansas City for our great fans, or not wanting to be a part of our organization. Our people have succeeded in large part because they display an unwavering commitment to win here in Kansas City.

This is the example of our president, Dan Glass. He has a heart for others and uses his influence to help many in need. Dan has great respect for the game of baseball and understands the special role the Royals play in bringing joy to the lives of others.

I revel in thinking about Dan on that stage around second base at Kauffman Stadium after we won the American League championship, with his dad, owner David Glass, holding the American League championship trophy, knowing that they were extremely patient in our building process. They stuck with us, as former longtime Royals groundskeeper George Toma would say, "and then some."

During the postseason, the Glass family went well beyond what would be expected of owners of any professional sports franchise by allowing our families to experience the postseason. Usually, key front-office personnel and perhaps a spouse are allowed to travel to postseason games. The same for players. The Glass family made sure we did everything we could to make the experience as special as possible for our families — players and the baseball operations staff. So we took as many people as we could to Chicago at the end of September for a possible clinching weekend, and then to Anaheim, Baltimore, and

San Francisco. It's difficult to put into words how much that meant to all of us. That is a great testament to the support we've received from the entire Glass family, especially Mr. Glass and Dan.

I hope that our team reflects the values, core principles, and character of the Glass family and the Kansas City community. We want this baseball team to be a reflection of our great city and fans. We have tried our best to raise our players with that in mind. One of the main reasons this city and baseball fans around the world enjoyed watching our

As much as I love the Royals, I've always said that my team is at home. I couldn't imagine doing what I'm doing without this team: (from left) Marianne, Robert, Ashley, and Avery.
Photo courtesy of Dayton Moore

team play was because our guys played hard, played for one another, and sincerely appreciated our fans.

We understand the role of this baseball team in the Kansas City community. The Royals have brought families together and helped heal broken hearts. Our run in 2014 perhaps took people's minds away from chemotherapy treatments or other illnesses and afflictions. This is the primary role a baseball team can play in a community. We understand that, at the end of the day, it's about more than a season.

C YOU IN THE MAJOR LEAGUES FOUNDATION

Inspiring Hope, Meeting Needs

DAYTON MOORE
Founder
www.cyitml.com

*Supporting youth baseball, education, families in crisis,
faith-based programs*

*For more information on the variety of ways to donate and
support the foundation, please contact:*

C YOU IN THE MAJOR LEAGUES FOUNDATION
c/o The National Christian Foundation Heartland
706 N. Lindenwood Dr.
Olathe, KS 66220
913-310-0279

"DEAR DAYTON..."

Each season I receive letters from fans, and I'm thankful that so many people reach out to me. That number skyrocketed after our team's incredible postseason run in 2014. The letters showed me how special the season was to our fans for numerous reasons. Although we've omitted the names, here are excerpts from a few of my favorites.

This one is from one of our season-ticket holders:

Thank you! I am 67 years old and remember watching Mickey Mantle, Yogi Berra, and other greats at the old [Municipal] stadium during the 1950s.... In all of these years, in all of the games I have attended, the Royals' win over the A's in the wild-card game was the most electrifying sports event I have EVER attended.... Thank you for creating the opportunity for this "game of the ages" to be played in our city.... Thank you, Dayton, for coming to Kansas City and having the perseverance to stick around when the negative criticism would have opened the door for weaker leaders to depart. Several years ago I stood next to you in Surprise, Arizona, and you told me there were five or six players on the field who would take us back to the top—you were so right. Thanks and God Bless!

From a fan in Chapmansboro, Tennessee:

I am writing to offer my congratulations for a tremendous 2014 season. I also offer my deepest thanks to you,

Ned Yost, the Royals organization, and the ballplayers for making baseball fun and exciting again. This TEAM was unselfish, clutch, and plays with Little League type enthusiasm.… This TEAM has captured four more fans in [our] household! We were glued to each game from the wild-card to Game 7 of the Series. This TEAM plays the game in a way that my 11- and 8-year-old sons can emulate. You have role models on your roster from top to bottom. Few, if any other, teams can say that. While it would have been rewarding to capture the World Series trophy, I think that this Royals TEAM captured something bigger and better. You all really did capture the hearts of baseball fans across the nation. It seemed as if nearly everyone watching these playoffs were pulling for KC. There is no doubt in my mind as to why, either. This TEAM plays the game the way it is supposed to be played, the players are genuine, and America saw that. My hat is off to all of you.

This one is from a fan in Lees Summit, Missouri. He opens the letter by thanking us and saying how his wife lost her mother to liver disease and her father to cancer in a three-week period from late August to mid-September. His wife wasn't a huge baseball fan:

…However, after the loss of her parents, she would sit with me and watch bits and pieces of the playoff chase down the final stretch. It was a way to take her mind off of things for a while—basically a light-hearted distraction. But once they made the wild-card game she was "all-in." We watched every inning of the postseason together from then on, and even made it to World Series Games 2 & 7.… I've rarely seen her as happy as when the Royals took Game 2 at Kauffman. It was simply amazing to see her smile again.… These young men helped our family through a very tough grieving period and provided healing in ways they don't even know.... Celebrating together with every Royals win was exactly what we needed to help us deal with the pain.

From a fan in Palmdale, California:

Living in Southern California, I decided to treat myself and my son to a joint birthday present and bought two tickets to the ALDS Game 2 in Anaheim. It was the first playoff game I'd ever been to in my life, and it was amazing from BP to the celebration after the game behind KC's dugout. The suspense, the defense (Dyson's throw), Ventura's pitching, and Hosmer's laser bomb are memories I'll always have. It was one of the best nights of my life, and to hear my son (who I thought was sleeping on the ride home) say, "Dad, I can't believe what we just saw," well, that was pretty cool....

Hold your head up high, Dayton. You guys made us all SO proud and gave us a ride we'll never forget. And I'm confident we'll be back. Thanks again and God bless you and your family.

This one is from a fan in Shawnee, Kansas, who wrote an incredibly heartfelt letter about his mother's battle with cancer. She was diagnosed in January 2014 and lost the fight in August. However, the family was able to take her to a Royals game during the season — one of her wishes:

That night, in my mind, the game was played entirely for her. Sports falls very nicely in the entertainment industry, but at least for this evening it meant so much more. I got to watch my mother chew sunflower seeds, spit the shells into a cup (and as THE definition of a lady this was a very,

very rare sight); she helped herself to peanuts and enjoyed a couple sips of beer though she was heavily medicated.... I wanted to write to express my thanks for that evening. As I said, attending a Royals baseball game was a request she made, and we made certain she was at Kauffman for at least one, which turned out to be her last and final game. As we wheeled her out of the stadium, she looked at us and said, "We should do this next year." Of course next year is never guaranteed to any of us. Please at least know that for one night, sports did not fall in the entertainment realm. Baseball once again replenished her energy and again touched her soul; and the Royals played for a lady who lived as close to a blameless life as we flawed mortals can.... So, in the spirit of my mother and behalf of my siblings, I say a very gracious thank you.

ABOUT THE AUTHORS

DAYTON MOORE became the sixth general manager in Royals history on June 8, 2006. Under Moore's leadership, the Royals built one of the best farm systems in baseball en route to reaching the postseason for the first time in 29 years as they won the 2014 American League championship by setting a major league record with eight straight wins. After the season, the Royals were selected as the *Baseball America* "Organization of the Year" for just the second time since the publication started the award in 1982, and Moore was awarded the "Executive of the Year" by Major League Baseball (GIBBY Awards) as well as the Kansas City Sports Commission. Moore, a native of Wichita, Kansas, was elected to the State of Kansas' Baseball Hall of Fame and named Kansan of the Year by the Native Sons and Daughters of Kansas. Moore was also tabbed Alumnus of the Year by George Mason University. Before joining the Royals, Moore worked in various capacities in player development for the Atlanta Braves from 1994 to 2006, after working as an assistant baseball coach at George Mason University from 1990 to 1994. In 2013 Moore started the C You in the Major Leagues Foundation to support youth baseball, education, families in crisis, and faith-based programs and organizations. (All author profits from the sale of this book go to the foundation.) Moore and his wife, Marianne, live in Leawood, Kansas. They have two daughters, Ashley and Avery, and a son, Robert.

MATT FULKS started his journalism career while attending Lipscomb University in Nashville, Tennessee, when his baseball career was cut short due to a lack of ability. He is the author/coauthor of more than 20 books, including *Out of the Blue*, about the 2014 Royals, *100 Things Royals Fans Should Know & Do Before They Die*, and multiple projects with Hall of Fame broadcaster Denny Matthews. He lives in the Kansas City area with his wife, their three children, his midlife crisis Jeep, and a Weimaraner named after Elvis. Sort of. More info is available at MattFulks.com (about Matt's books, not the dog).